Mind Joggers!

5- to 15-Minute Activities that Make Kids Think

Susan S. Petreshene

Illustrated by Patricia A. Fox

The Center for Applied Research in Education, Inc.
West Nyack, New York 10995

**To my husband, Vic,
our children, Kathy and Steve,
and my mother, Josephine Habbe.**

Library of Congress Cataloging-in-Publication Data

Petreshene, Susan S.
  Mind Joggers!

  1. Creative activities and seat work—Handbooks,
manuals, etc. 2 Cognition—Study and teaching
(Primary) I. Title.
LB1537.P46 1985   370.15'2   85-17171

ISBN 0-87628-583-3

ABOUT THIS RESOURCE

For most teachers unplanned-for extra minutes occur from time to time, even during the most organized school day. You might have spare minutes before recess, lunch, or some special event, or when a lesson finishes early. These few minutes are not enough for a formal lesson but are sufficient for a worthwhile activity, provided you have one right at your fingertips that requires no preparation and uses simple, readily available materials like paper and pencil or chalkboard and chalk.

Mind Joggers! 5- to 15-Minute Activities that Make Kids Think has been designed to fill such time gaps with *quality* activities. Included are "Total Group Activities," for use with the entire class, and "Individual or Partner Activities," for students who complete assignments early or who want extra challenges.

Here is an interesting mix of 153 "quick" activities for kindergarten through grade six, in four major subject and skill areas:

> Thinking and Reasoning Activities (30 activities)
>
> Math Activities (59 activities)
>
> Language and Writing Activities (51 activities)
>
> Listening and Remembering Activities (13 activities)

A number of the activities stimulate creative thinking, rather than have the students search for a single right answer. Many of the activities parallel standardized test items and provide practice in the specific thought patterns required by such tests. Others can be used to introduce a new concept or to review a previously taught skill. Most of the activities can serve as extensions of regular class work, and many can be used as homework assignments that require students to think and reason. Most important, *all* are meant to be productive skill-reinforcers or extenders.

Whether you are a teacher, student teacher, substitute teacher, or classroom aide, whenever you find yourself faced with unexpected free time you can open this resource and quickly find a ready-to-use activity. The handy Activities/Skills Index on pages v-x provides a convenient listing of all activities by subject matter, skill area, grade level, and group size.

For each activity you'll find the same easy-to-use format that provides:

- activity number and title
- subject and skill reinforced
- appropriate grade levels for use
- appropriate classroom groups for use
- complete list of materials needed
- step-by-step activity directions
- adaptations for other groups
- activity variations
- resource lists of words, questions, problems, and topics
- complete answer keys
- follow-up activities

For example, if you wish to use the time to develop thinking skills, but on short notice you don't have time to create a challenging activity or search through your files for one, you can select one from the thirty activities in the Thinking and Reasoning section of this book. In no time at all your students can be productively using this time on activities like "Above/Below the Ground" (Making Quick Decisions) and "Seasons in Hiding" (Logic Skills).

If you keep this resource book handy, it will help you make each of your spare minutes count. I hope you and your classes enjoy it!

Susan S. Petreshene

ACTIVITIES/SKILLS INDEX

| | TOTAL GROUP ACTIVITY | INDIVIDUAL ACTIVITY | PARTNER ACTIVITY | |

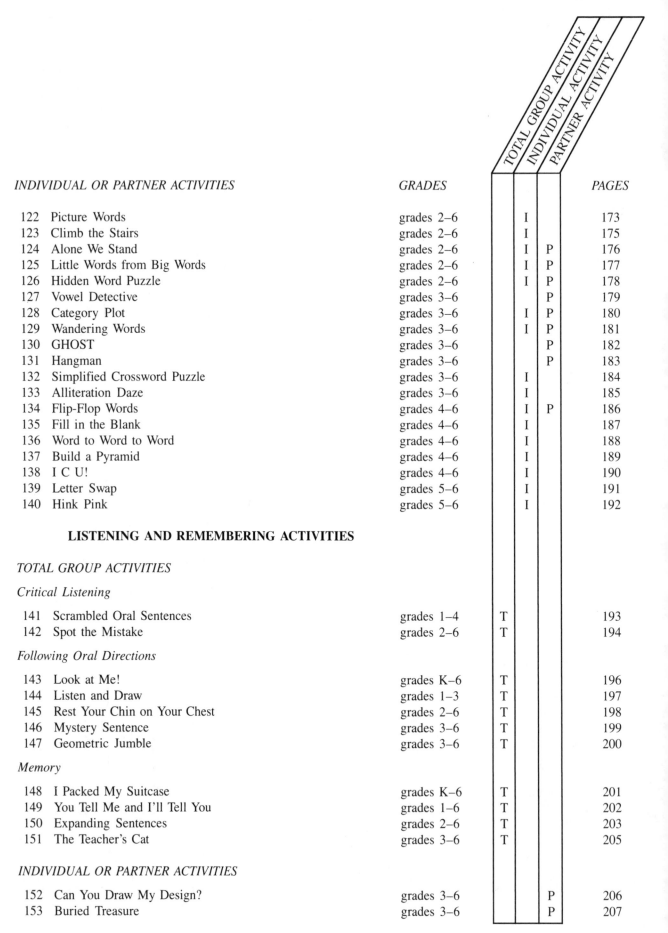

SUGGESTIONS FOR USING THESE ACTIVITIES MOST EFFECTIVELY

Mind Joggers! 5- to 15-Minute Activities That Make Kids Think is a collection of 153 "quick" activities to develop thinking skills in students from kindergarten through grade six. Here is a great variety of activities, both traditional and new, that are ready to go at a minute's notice to help students spend spare time productively.

This unique resource is divided into four major skill areas:

> Thinking and Reasoning Activities
>
> Math Activities
>
> Language and Writing Activities
>
> Listening and Remembering Activities

Each section is subdivided into "Total Group Activities" and "Individual or Partner Activities." In each of these sections, the activities are designed primarily for use with the groups designated in the boxes at the top of the page, but most provide adaptations for other groups. The Activities/Skills Index on pages v–x provides a simple keying system so you can select activities appropriate to specific group sizes quickly and easily.

The activities within each subsection are sequenced from lower grade to upper grade so you can select the activity most suitable to your students' level. If the level of an activity changes from the Total Group Activity to the Individual or Partner Activity, the new level is indicated next to the heading "Adaptation for an Individual Student (Grades X–X)."

As you look through the Activities/Skills Index, you will see a few traditional activities such as "Ghost" and "Hangman." These have been included as a refresher for game rules and to make the book a comprehensive resource of worthwhile activities.

Total Group Activities

When using the Total Group Activities, you may want to consider using one or more of the following implementation suggestions:

1. Select a topic, such as "Geometry," and work sequentially through the activities in that section as spare time arises.

2. Alternate using activities from several different sections. Leave markers indicating where to resume when you return to a specific section so you won't repeat activities.

3. Select a specific activity to be used as an introduction to a new skill or as a review of previously learned concepts.

4. When writing lesson plans, familiarize yourself with several activities that you feel will benefit your students and mark these for ready access during the week.

5. Allot a regular time period for using the activities. You will find that there will be much class interaction and involvement during the five to fifteen minutes of activity time, resulting in an enjoyable break in the routine for both you and your students. This type of break is especially effective when it follows intensive academic studies, silent reading periods, or active periods such as recess or physical education.

Some of the Total Group Activities may be adapted for use by individual students or by partners. These activities have been coded for these uses at the top right-hand corner of the page. Necessary materials are listed (if different from those of the Total Group Activity), and adaptations are provided.

Individual or Partner Activities

These activities have been designed to fill a need different from that of the Total Group Activities. Here are productive time-fillers for students who complete their assignments early or who want extra challenges.

Each of the Individual or Partner Activities can be introduced to the entire class in a few minutes either at the beginning of the day or prior to a specific related assignment. In some cases students may already be familiar with the activity; however, the total group introduction should ensure that everyone understands the procedures. Then, when a student unexpectedly finishes work ahead of time, you can use these activities to challenge or reinforce appropriate skills for that specific student.

Individual Activities often result in a puzzle, problem, or other product that can serve as a challenge for other students during their free time. For example, if one student has built a "Word to Word to Word" puzzle (Activity 136), his or her riddle and puzzle directions are written on paper with the answer on the reverse side and left for others to solve. You may wish to designate a box, file folder, or bulletin board space where challenges may be placed. Or you may compile these challenges in a special puzzle book for individual or whole-class use.

Keep track of the Individual or Partner Activities that have been introduced to the whole class by maintaining a posted list of these activities. By glancing at this list, both you and your students can quickly answer the question "What can I do now?"

Format Designed for Easiest Use

Mind Joggers! has been formatted so that you can quickly select appropriate activities for on-the-spot use. The Activities/Skills Index helps you find suitable activities for particular groups of students in specific subject areas. The format of each activity also helps you decide at a glance if it is best for your needs at the moment. And you can flip from one activity to another without having to refer to material elsewhere in the book. Even when directions remain the same from one activity to another, they have been repeated to make each activity a self-contained unit.

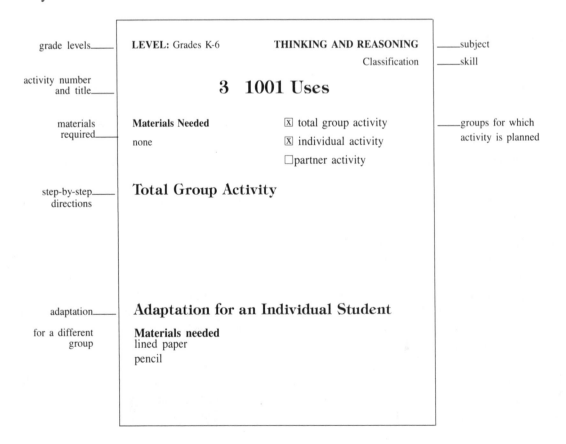

As shown in the sample activity format on p xii, each activity begins with the subject and skill in the upper right corner of the page. The upper left corner gives the grade level designation. At the top of the page you'll find the activity number and title. Below it is a complete list of all materials needed (if any) and boxes checked to indicate the groups with which the activity may be used.

Then each activity is clearly explained, step by step, for the primary group for which it is intended. Adaptations for other groups then follow the primary use. Variations show how an activity can be altered for variety, and Follow-Up Activities extend the activity in other time slots.

Finally, resource lists of words, problems, topics, and so on, are provided. Answer keys are supplied whenever possible, printed in distinctive boldface type for easy visibility. In most cases, however, any answer that can be supported by good reasoning should be accepted. The supplied answers are noted as samples only.

Markers and Notes

Regardless of how you use the activities, a few well-placed markers are invaluable in getting the most from this book. These make it possible for you, or for a substitute teacher or classroom aide, to have a variety of activities marked for use at a moment's notice.

Markers are also helpful for tagging activities with resource lists. The words on these lists are sequenced from easiest to most difficult, so they should be scanned to determine where to begin with your students. Where to start and stop can be indicated on a marker. Also, when you use part of a list you can place a marker where you stop so you can resume at that place later.

You may also wish to make brief notes on the activity page regarding your students' responses and reactions. These notes will be quite useful when working with students the following year.

How to Decide Who Goes First in Partner Activities

For partner activities it is helpful to have a quick way to determine who goes first. Suggest to students that they use either of the following methods.

ODD/EVEN: One student chooses "odd" and the other "even." Each student puts a hand behind his back and together they silently count "1-2-3." On "3," both students thrust a hand in front of them with one to five fingers showing. If the total number of fingers is odd, the player who chose "odd" goes first. If the total is even, the other player gets the first turn.

WHICH HAND? One student puts both hands behind his or her back and places a small object in one hand. Both hands are then held in front of the other player, who tries to guess which hand contains the object. If correct, that player goes first. Otherwise the person holding the object goes first.

How to Teach the "Trick" Behind Each "Computation Magic Trick"

One special note concerns the Math subsection "Computation Magic Tricks." Encourage the students to use these tricks with family and friends and unknowingly they will receive added practice with basic computation skills. Also challenge them to try to discover *why* each of the tricks works. The "magic formula" varies from trick to trick, but in each case it involves nothing more than doing a series of things to a number and then later undoing them. For instance, if 53 has been added to the original number, at some point this amount will need to be subtracted. It may be done at one time, or it may be accomplished in several separate steps (subtract 25, subtract 25, subtract 3). Likewise, if the original number has been multiplied by 6, it will be necessary to divide by six in order to get back to the starting number.

Discuss this "doing" and "undoing" process with students and make a chart that shows what happens to the original number during each step of the magic trick. The following chart is an analysis of Activity 81, "Back to Square One." With practice, students will learn to analyze magic tricks on their own.

1. In step one, the student picks a number. For this explanation we will let X equal the number.	X
2. Next, 6 is added to the number, resulting in:	$X + 6$
3. The new number is then multiplied by 4.	$4(X + 6) = 4X + 24$
4. Now the student adds 7.	$4X + 24 + 7 = 4X + 31$
5. This number is multiplied by 2. At this point, the original number has been multiplied by 8, plus 62 has been added to it. It is now time to begin the "undoing" process, so we can get rid of the excess numbers.	$2(4X + 31) = 8X + 62$
6. In step six, 62 is subtracted. What remains is 8 times the original number.	$8X + 62 - 62 = 8X$
7. Now all that is necessary is to get rid of the multiple of 8. This is accomplished by dividing by 8. Voila! The undoing process is complete and we're back to the original number the student chose.	$\dfrac{8X}{8} = X$

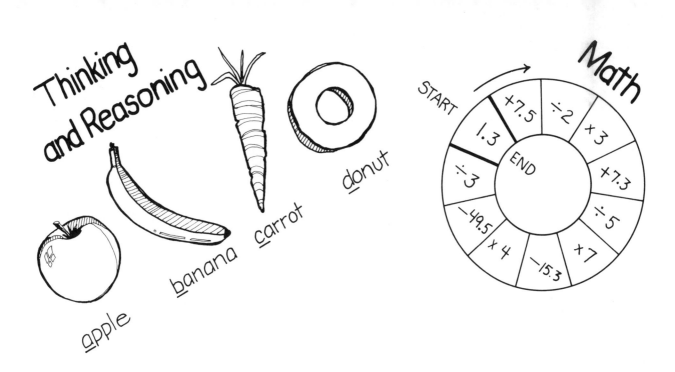

Thinking and Reasoning

apple

banana carrot donut

Math

START +7.5 ÷2 x3 +7.3 ÷5 x7 −15.3 x4 −49.5 ÷3 1.3 END

Activities

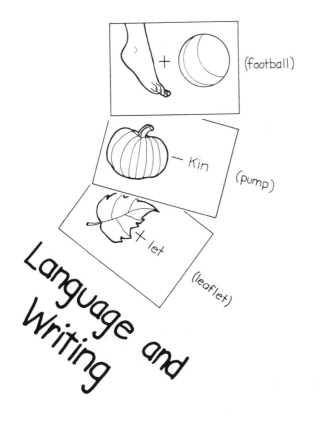

+ ⚽ (football)

− Kin (pump)

+ let (leaflet)

Language and Writing

Listening and Remembering

1   HOW MANY CAN YOU NAME?
(CATEGORIES FOR BRAINSTORMING)

Materials needed
none

☒ total group activity
☒ individual activity
☒ partner activity

Total Group Activity

When brainstorming classification topics, it is fun to challenge students to see how many different answers they can discover. Initial responses are invariably the common ones, but as the list grows the children are forced to stretch their minds for more unusual items. It is always fascinating to watch this thinking process unfold.

Give students a category from the following list and ask them to name as many items as they can think of that fit within that classification. Accept any answer that can be backed with logical reasoning. Tally the total number on the chalkboard or hold up a finger for each response. Duplicate responses do not count. You will find that by calling attention to the importance of listening, students soon hear repetitions as quickly, if not more quickly, than you do. What's more, they invariably can say who it was who originally gave the response! Use the "Warm-Up Topics" until students are comfortable with the process, then move on to the more challenging "Brain-Stretchers."

This activity can always be counted on for as instant time-filler to stretch creative thinking.

Adaptation for an Individual Student

Materials needed
lined paper
pencil

Name a topic from the following list and have the student list as many items as he or she can think of that fit within the category.

Partner Adaptation

Materials needed
lined paper
pencil
clock *or* timer

Partners select a category from the following list and take turns naming items that fit within that classification. When no more words can be thought of within a certain time period the person who named the last item receives one point. A new category should then be selected and the procedure repeated. The winner is the first student who earns five points or who has the higher score at the end of a designated time period. The words need not be written; paper and pencil are for scorekeeping only.

Variation: This activity can easily be made a silent activity by having players take turns writing words that belong in the designated category. Scoring remains the same.

Warm-Up Brainstorming Topics

1. zoo animals
2. things with wheels
3. things you can see in a classroom
4. things that are hot
5. activities you can do outside
6. pets
7. furniture
8. fruits
9. sounds made by animals
10. things you can drink
11. farm animals
12. things you can smell
13. things you might see if you looked out your front window at home
14. things that are sweet
15. vegetables
16. words that begin with m or t
17. things that taste good
18. kitchen utensils
19. things that are round
20. breakfast foods
21. things you might find in a living room
22. clothing
23. wild animals
24. things that have handles
25. things made of plastic
26. types of tools
27. things with motors
28. things made of wood
29. things that roll
30. words that begin with s or r
31. types of sports
32. things made of glass
33. means of travel
34. things that stretch
35. types of ships or boats
36. things you can wear on your head

BRAIN-STRETCHERS

1. animals:
     with tails
     without tails
2. games that can be played by:
     one person alone
     more than one person
3. things that are sticky
4. small creatures
5. fruits and vegetables that have a part that is not eaten (**Tell what part or parts are not eaten.**)
6. things you can ride
7. characteristics that make a person a good friend
8. animals that are good swimmers (**Tell *how* each swims.**)
9. words associated with the ocean
10. places to go
11. foods that might be:
     peeled
     mashed
     squeezed
     cracked
     husked
12. animals that:
     bite or claw to protect themselves
     do not bite or claw (**Tell how each protects itself.**)
13. colors
14. words associated with a rainy day
15. water sports that can be done in:
     the ocean
     a small lake
16. animals that:
     peck
     gnaw
17. things that are slippery
18. things you can find in the forest
19. things that can be heard
20. things you can drive

21. things that come in:
    a jar
    a bag
    pairs
22. things that float
23. animals that build nests
24. things you might see in a park
25. things that are soft
26. things you would find in or near the water
27. things that can be read
28. fruits or vegetables that have:
    one pit or seed
    many pits or seeds
    no pits or seeds
29. things you might find in someone's garage
30. words that sound like what they mean (**For example:** *clang, fizz,* **or** *snap.* **You may want to introduce the word** *onomatopoeia.)*
31. kinds of birds
32. plants that live:
    for a short time or only one season
    for a long time
33. things that are smooth
34. animals that live both in the water and on land
35. musical instruments

36. kinds of dogs
37. things that have a shell
38. action words or words that show movement
39. kinds of fish
40. words associated with weather
41. occupations
42. ways to communicate
43. words of measurement
44. types of shelter
45. words associated with fairy tales
46. precious stones
47. types of insects
48. things that go up and down
49. makes of cars
50. types of metals
51. states in the United States
52. kinds of trees
53. countries in the world
54. inventors
55. explorers
56. rivers
57. mountains

2 MISMATCH

Materials needed
none

☒ total group activity
☒ individual activity
☐ partner activity

Total Group Activity

Read a group of four or five words from the following list and have the students pick out the one word that does not fit with the others. Read the words in each group slowly the first time, then repeat them slowly. The repetition and slow pace are important because the students need to listen carefully and check the validity of their original answers. Ask students to raise their hands to give the answer *after* you have read the words twice. When answers are given, students should explain their reasoning to provide examples for those who are less secure. Any answer backed by logical reasoning should be accepted whether or not it appears in this book as the answer.

This is a good activity to use when you want children to settle down after an active period.

Adaptation for an Individual Student

Materials needed
lined paper (6″ x 9″ for class book)
pencil

The student lists five words on a piece of paper, four of which go together in some logical way. One of the words should not fit with the others but should have some common elements. Explain that if the mismatched word is too different there will be no challenge in solving the puzzle.

The answer and its explanation should be written on the reverse side of the paper. For example: (front side) dog, gopher, cat, guinea pig; (reverse side) gopher. It is not a pet.

When a sufficient number of these papers have been collected, they can be assembled into an interesting and stimulating class puzzle book to be used individually or as a total group activity.

Find the Mismatch

1. store, bank, furniture, grocery **(furniture—not a building)**
2. kitten, cow, canary, dog **(cow—not a household pet)**
3. carrot, peach, potato, green bean **(peach—not a vegetable)**
4. lion, giraffe, cat, monkey **(cat—not a zoo animal)**
5. chicken, turkey, duck, canary **(canary—not raised for food)**
6. swings, blocks, slides, teeter-totters **(blocks—not playground equipment)**
7. wrench, hammer, nail, screwdriver **(nail—not a tool)**
8. baseball, bingo, football, basketball **(bingo—not a game using a ball)**
9. stop, start, end, finish **(start—not a word that means "to stop")**
10. shutter, carpet, chimney, door **(carpet—not a part of a house's structure)**
11. person, shoulders, knees, neck **(person—not a part of a person)**
12. inch, foot, ruler, yard **(ruler—not a unit of measurement)**

13. ice cream, milk, cake, pudding   **(milk—not a dessert)**

14. sledding, snow, rain, sleet   **(sledding—not a form of precipitation)**

15. bird, plane, car, balloon   **(car—does not fly or float in the air)**

16. road, sidewalk, freeway, street   **(sidewalk—cars do not travel on it)**

17. slice, chop, ax, carve   **(ax—not a method of cutting food)**

18. gutter, sidewalk, river, curb   **(river—not part of a paved area)**

19. kitten, cat, fawn, gosling   **(cat—not a baby animal)**

20. book, pamphlet, pencil,   **(pencil—not material to be read)**
    newspaper

21. ant, snail, beetle, bee   **(snail—not an insect)**

22. whale, octopus, kangaroo,   **(kangaroo—not an aquatic animal)**
    dolphin

23. excited, frightened, scared,   **(excited—not a word that describes being**
    terrified   **frightened)**

24. parakeet, robin, canary,   **(robin—a bird that has not been domesticated)**
    cockatoo

25. ocean, beach, pond, lake   **(beach—not a body of water)**

26. quarterback, catcher, shortstop,   **(quarterback—not a player on a baseball team)**
    pitcher

27. sword, armor, rifle, cannon   **(armor—not a weapon)**

28. Florida, Chicago, Illinois,   **(Chicago—not a state)**
    California

29. huge, horrendous, enormous,   **(horrendous—not a word that describes**
    gigantic   **something large)**

30. dog, gopher, cat, guinea pig   **(gopher—not a domesticated animal)**

31. cargo ship, canoe, wharf, sailboat   **(wharf—not a boat)**

32. guitar, clarinet, piano, violin   **(clarinet—not a stringed instrument)**

33. orchid, ivy, carnation, tulip   **(ivy—not a flowering plant)**

34. orange, grapefruit, peach, lemon   **(peach—not a citrus fruit)**

35. paint, brush, palette, artist   **(artist—not a tool or material used by a painter)**

36. Pekingese, dachshund, Siamese,   **(Siamese—not a breed of dog)**
    Dalmatian

37. jewels, sparkling, glittering,   **(jewels—not a word that means "shining")**
    shining

38. ruby, emerald, gold, sapphire   **(gold—not a jewel)**

39. water, lemonade, ice cube,   **(ice cube—not a beverage)**
    orange juice

40. department store, motel,   **(department store—not a place where people live)**
    condominium, apartment

41. request, demand, beg, ask   **(demand—not a word that means "to ask")**

42. tote, transport, carry, hoist   **(hoist—not a word that means "to carry")**

43. iceberg, water, glacier, ice cube   **(water—not frozen)**

44. pickles, jam, potato chips, olives   **(potato chips—not a food commonly found in**
                                            jars)

45. forest, plateau, valley, mountain   **(forest—not a landform)**

3   1001 USES

Materials needed:
none

☒ total group activity
☒ individual activity
☐ partner activity

Total Group Activity

Lots of creative thinking takes place during this activity in which you ask students to name as many ways as they can think of to use an item from the following list. It is important to accept all reasonable responses, and to ask students to explain their answers if you do not understand their reasoning.

A student once said that a broom could be used to break a window. This appeared to be nothing more than a silly response. However, when asked to explain, she said, "If there were a fire, you could use a broom to break the window and get out."

It may be necessary to remind students periodically that they should think of practical answers, not ones intended to get laughs. At the same time, encourage them to think of uses for items that differ from the true use.

Adaptation for an Individual Student

Materials needed
lined paper
pencil

Name something from the following list and have the student list as many ways as he or she can think of to use the item.

How Many Ways Can You Think of to Use

1. a cup
2. a light bulb
3. a button
4. a bird cage
5. a piece of paper
6. an old bathtub
7. a broom
8. a ladder
9. a brick
10. a candle
11. a walnut
12. a hat
13. a broken clock
14. a tea kettle
15. a bead
16. a nail
17. a wastebasket
18. an old parachute
19. a tree branch
20. a chair
21. a needle
22. a block
23. a tire
24. an umbrella
25. a sock
26. a book
27. an old school bus that doesn't run
28. a trunk
29. an old typewriter
30. a pencil
31. a barrel
32. a plate
33. a pillow
34. a spoon
35. a ring

4   A TYPE OF —

Materials needed
none

☒ total group activity
☒ individual activity
☐ partner activity

Total Group Activity

Name an object from the following list and have students tell you what category it belongs in. For example: "Apple is a type of ..." (**fruit**); "A sword is a type of ..." (**weapon**).

Encourage students to be as specific as possible when naming categories. This, of course, will vary according to the age and ability level of your students. If *apple* is identified as a kind of food, acknowledge the answer, but ask if the student can give a word that describes the category more precisely. Possible answers have been listed below; however, in many cases there will be more than one correct response. Accept all responses that seem appropriate.

Adaptation for an Individual Student

Materials needed
lined paper
pencil

The student makes a list of as many objects as he or she can think of and indicates the category or categories in which each belongs.

This Is a Type of —

1. carrot is a type of	**(vegetable)**
2. desk is a type of	**(furniture)**
3. water is a type of	**(liquid)**
4. lion is a type of	**(wild animal)**
5. shirt is a type of	**(clothing)**
6. grocery is a type of	**(store)**
7. checkers is a type of	**(game)**
8. blocks are a type of	**(toy)**
9. canary is a type of	**(bird)**
10. purple is a type of	**(color)**
11. hammer is a type of	**(tool)**
12. daffodil is a type of	**(flower)**
13. dog is a type of	**(pet)**
14. rooster is a type of	**(farm animal)**
15. dandelion is a type of	**(weed)**
16. football is a type of	**(sport)**
17. lemonade is a type of	**(drink)**

18. inch is a type of   **(measurement)**
19. trout is a type of   **(fish)**
20. barn is a type of   **(building)**
21. rain is a type of   **(weather)**
22. pheasant is a type of   **(bird)**
23. canoe is a type of   **(boat)**
24. fawn is a type of   **(baby animal)**
25. tractor is a type of   **(farm equipment)**
26. weeping willow is a type of   **(tree)**
27. cake is a type of   **(dessert)**
28. dime is a type of   **(coin)**
29. mosquito is a type of   **(insect)**
30. poodle is a type of   **(dog)**
31. pancakes are a type of   **(breakfast food)**
32. bus is a type of   **(transportation)**
33. crying is a type of   **(emotion)**
34. cottage cheese is a type of   **(dairy product)**
35. newspaper is a type of   **(reading material)**
36. thistle is a type of   **(weed)**
37. octopus is a type of   **(sea animal)**
38. cello is a type of   **(instrument)**
39. chrysanthemum is a type of   **(flower)**
40. emerald is a type of   **(jewel/precious stone)**
41. being frightened is a type of   **(emotion)**
42. copperhead is a type of   **(snake)**
43. jigsaw is a type of   **(tool)**
44. spatula is a type of   **(kitchen utensil)**
45. magenta is a type of   **(color)**
46. slide is a type of   **(playground equipment)**
47. cannon is a type of   **(weapon)**
48. snake is a type of   **(reptile)**
49. cactus is a type of   **(desert plant)**
50. gold is a type of   **(precious metal)**
51. persimmon is a type of   **(fruit)**
52. salamander is a type of   **(amphibian)**
53. pencil is a type of   **(writing instrument)**
54. rugby is a type of   **(sport)**
55. piranha is a type of   **(fish)**
56. venison is a type of   **(meat)**
57. chalet is a type of   **(house)**
58. clavicord is a type of   **(instrument)**
59. spaghetti is a type of   **(pasta)**
60. mountain is a type of   **(geological feature)**

5   ALPHABETICAL CLASSIFICATION

Materials needed
none

☒ total group activity
☒ individual activity
☒ partner activity

Total Group Activity

Select one of the categories from the following list and have students name items within the category that begin with each letter of the alphabet in order. For example, if you chose "things in a classroom," students might name: apples, books, chalkboards, desks, erasers, and so on, through the letter Z.

You may find that certain letters (especially *x* and some of the vowels) need to be omitted when you play this game. Ground rules on unacceptable words can be discussed before you begin the game, or you can stop and talk about specific situations as they occur. For example, for the game "things in a classroom," students will want to know whether they may use the names of people in the classroom.

This activity is especially fun when students are challenged to try to go through the entire alphabet, skipping no more than two or three letters.

Adaptation for an Individual Student

Materials needed
lined paper
pencil

apple   banana   carrot   donut

The student selects a topic from the following list and writes a word for each letter of the alphabet.

Partner Adaptation

Materials needed
lined paper
pencil

Partners select a category from the following list and work together writing a word for each letter of the alphabet.

Create an Alphabetical Classification for This

1. animals (**ant, bear, cat, dog**...)
2. things in a classroom (**atlas, ball, chair, door**...)
3. foods (**apricot, banana, cereal, donut**...)
4. items you can buy, other than food (**automobile, balloon, candle, drum**...)
5. things that have a round or curved part (**anchor, ball, cup, doorknob**...)
6. musical instruments (**accordion, banjo, cello, drum**...)
7. things in a house (**antenna, bedroom, cupboard, dresser**...)
8. occupations (**accountant, bricklayer, carpenter, doctor**...)
9. items in a kitchen (**apron, blender, coffee pot, dish**...)
10. what you might do on vacation (**archery, bowl, camp, drive**...)
11. things in a garage (**ax, board, car, drill**...)
12. words that describe a person (**active, bouncy, careful, daring**...)

6 WHICH COMES FIRST: THE CHICKEN OR THE EGG?

Materials needed
none

☒ total group activity
☒ individual activity
☐ partner activity

Total Group Activity

Name a group of items from the following list and have students try to discover a way to sequence the words as they listen. For example, if you said, "lemon, watermelon, grapefruit, orange," the words could be ordered according to size from smallest to largest or vice versa: lemon, orange, grapefruit, watermelon, or watermelon, grapefruit, orange, lemon.

Begin by reading the first three words in each group. When students can easily order three words, read groups of four words.

Note: One possible answer is given, but any logical sequence that can be explained by the student should be accepted. All sequences should be explained to permit broad exposure to the thinking of others.

Students consistently enjoy this activity and become very involved. You'll find that it is a fun way to practice listening, thinking, and reasoning skills.

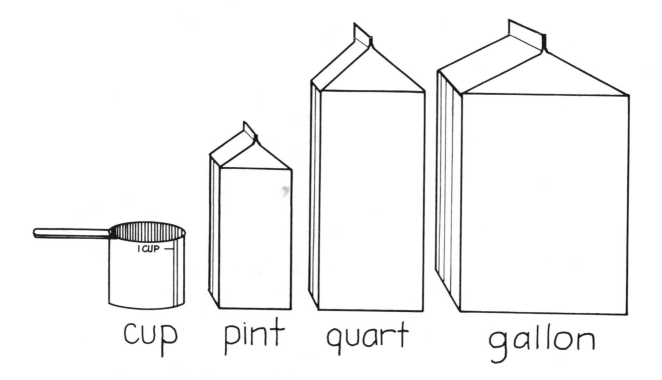

cup   pint   quart   gallon

Adaptation for an Individual Student

Materials needed
lined paper (6″ x 9″ for class book)
pencil

On a piece of paper the student lists four words that can be sequenced in some way. The answer, along with the reasoning involved, should be written on the reverse side. When a sufficient number of papers have been collected, they can be assembled into a thought-provoking class puzzle book for individual or whole-class use.

Sequence These

1. pigeon, hummingbird, eagle, sparrow

   (**hummingbird, sparrow, pigeon, eagle—sizes from small to large**)

2. cow, dog, elephant, mouse

   (**mouse, dog, cow, elephant—sizes from small to large**)

3. year, day, month, week

   (**day, week, month, year—lengths of time from short to long**)

4. high school, college, elementary school, nursery school

   (**nursery school, elementary school, high school, college—sequence of educational schooling from low to high level**)

5. dime, penny, nickel, quarter

   (**penny, nickel, dime, quarter—values of money from small to large**)

6. million, hundred, thousand, billion

   (**hundred, thousand, million, billion—numbers from low to high**)

7. foot, inch, mile, yard

   (**inch, foot, yard, mile—lengths from small to large**)

8. wheat, dough, bread, flour

   (**wheat, flour, dough, bread—steps in baking process**)

9. rock, sand, pebble, boulder

   (**sand, pebble, rock, boulder—sizes from small to large**)

10. great-grandmother, child, mother, grandmother

    (**child, mother, grandmother, great-grandmother—ages from young to old**)

11. large, small, medium, gigantic

    (**small, medium, large, gigantic—sizes from small to large**)

12. dusk, morning, night, noon

    (**morning, noon, dusk, night—times of day from morning to night**)

13. teenager, child, infant, adult

    (**infant, child, teenager, adult—stages of human development from young to old**)

14. fall, summer, winter, spring

    (**summer, fall, winter, spring—seasons from summer to spring**)

15. minute, hour, second, day

    (**second, minute, hour, day—lengths of time from short to long**)

16. egg, adult, pupa, larva

    (**egg, larva, pupa, adult—stages of insect development from young to old**)

17. tens, thousands, hundreds, ones

(ones, tens, hundreds, thousands—place values from small to large)

18. pint, cup, quart, gallon

(cup, pint, quart, gallon—liquid capacities from small to large)

19. mouse, hawk, snake, grain

(grain, mouse, snake, hawk—food chain from beginning to end)

20. word, letter, paragraph, sentence

(letter, word, sentence, paragraph—parts of written communication from small to large)

21. floor, foundation, roof, frame

(foundation, floor, frame, roof—parts of a building from bottom to top)

22. Fourth of July, Thanksgiving, Halloween, New Year's Day

(New Year's Day, Fourth of July, Halloween, Thanksgiving—holidays from the beginning of the year to the end)

23. state, country, city, county

(city, county, state, country—geographic units in the United States from small to large)

24. electricity, water, light, dam

(water, dam, electricity, light—steps in making hydroelectricity from beginning to end)

25. legs, head, body, neck

(legs, body, neck, head—parts of a human body from bottom to top)

26. bread, baker, consumer, store

(baker, bread, store, consumer—steps in bread marketing from beginning to end)

27. rhubarb, carrot, celery, bean

(bean, carrot, celery, rhubarb—lengths from short to long)

28. Civil War, World War II, Revolutionary War, World War I

(Revolutionary War, Civil War, World War I, World War II—wars in historical order)

29. production, research, development, marketing

(research, development, production, marketing—steps in the marketing process)

30. decimeter, centimeter, millimeter, meter

(millimeter, centimeter, decimeter, meter—lengths from short to long)

7 WHAT'S MY CATEGORY?

Materials needed
¼ sheet of lined paper for each student
pencil for each student
clock *or* timer

[X] total group activity
[ ] individual activity
[X] partner activity

Total Group Activity

Before beginning this activity it is important to define the term *category*. Name a few categories with examples of items in each, such as "farm animals": cow, chicken, pig, goat; or "sports": baseball, football, soccer, hockey. When students understand the idea, provide a few minutes for each child to select a category and write five or six items in that category. Encourage them to choose a specific topic such as "farm animals" or "animals with backbones," rather than the broad category "animals."

Call on one student to begin reading his or her list of items *slowly*, pausing between each item. As soon as students think they know the category, they should raise their hands to give the answer. The student reading the list calls on students for the answer. If the answer is incorrect, the reader should continue with the list until the category is guessed. The first student to guess the category correctly becomes the next reader.

Partner Adaptation

Each partner selects a category and makes a list of five related words. One partner begins reading his or her list. The other student may guess one category after each word is read. When the category is correctly identified, the reader receives one point for each word remaining on the list. The students then reverse roles. The first person to earn fifteen points or the person who has the most points at the end of a designated time period wins.

Variation: This activity can easily be made a silent partner activity by having the first player *show* words on his or her list, one word at a time, allowing the other player to *write* a guess after each new clue is shown.

8   ABOVE/BELOW THE GROUND

Materials needed
none

☒ total group activity
☒ individual activity
☐ partner activity

Total Group Activity

Read the names of fruits and vegetables from the following list to the students. If the part we eat grows above the ground, have them raise their arms above their heads. If the part we eat grows below the ground, have them point both hands toward the ground.

Variations: Students may respond by putting hands up/hands down or thumbs up/thumbs down. Students who are uncertain should fold their arms.

Remind them to think before responding. To provide ample thinking time, after you read the word hold up your opened hand and silently count to five. They should indicate their answers when you close your fist.

Adaptation for an Individual Student

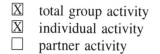

Materials needed
lined paper
pencil

The student draws a line down the middle of a piece of paper and labels the two sections "Above the Ground" and "Below the Ground." In the appropriate column, he or she lists as many fruits or vegetables as possible. The list provided for this activity may be used as an answer key.

Does it Grow above or below the Ground?

1. orange	**(above)**		18. turnip	**(below)**
2. tomato	**(above)**		19. apple	**(above)**
3. beet	**(below)**		20. avocado	**(above)**
4. strawberry	**(above)**		21. cabbage	**(above)**
5. carrot	**(below)**		22. horseradish	**(below)**
6. pear	**(above)**		23. cherry	**(above)**
7. cucumber	**(above)**		24. sugar beet	**(below)**
8. potato	**(below)**		25. date	**(above)**
9. cantaloupe	**(above)**		26. green pepper	**(above)**
10. peanut	**(below)**		27. radish	**(below)**
11. pumpkin	**(above)**		28. banana	**(above)**
12. green bean	**(above)**		29. cauliflower	**(above)**
13. celery	**(above)**		30. corn	**(above)**
14. onion	**(below)**		31. parsnip	**(below)**
15. squash	**(above)**		32. peach	**(above)**
16. broccoli	**(above)**		33. Brussels sprout	**(above)**
17. lettuce	**(above)**		34. garlic	**(below)**

9 THINGS YOU CAN CHANGE OR CANNOT CHANGE

Materials needed

Total Group Activity

Read the following list of phrases describing situations to the students. They have the power or ability to change some of the situations on the list, such as the brightness of a lamp, but cannot change others, such as how tall they are. Have them put their thumbs up if you read something they can change and point their thumbs down if it is something they cannot change.

Variations: Students may respond by sitting/standing or putting hands up/hands down.

Remind them to think before responding. To provide ample thinking time, after you read the word hold up your opened hand and silently count to five. They should respond when you close your fist.

Adaptation for an Individual Student

Materials needed
lined paper
pencil

The student draws a line down the middle of a piece of paper and labels the two sections "Can Change" and "Cannot Change." In the appropriate column, he or she lists as many items as possible for each of the categories.

Is It Something You Can Change or Cannot Change?

1. the clothes you wear	**(can change)**
2. the color of your eyes	**(cannot change)**
3. the weather	**(cannot change)**
4. how neat your room is	**(can change)**
5. the day of the week	**(cannot change)**
6. the people you play with	**(can change)**
7. the plants in your garden	**(can change)**
8. having to go to school	**(cannot change)**
9. the correct spelling of a word	**(cannot change)**
10. the food you eat	**(can change)**
11. how much something costs at the grocery store	**(cannot change)**
12. the games you play	**(can change)**
13. the number of hours in a day	**(cannot change)**
14. how well you write your name	**(can change)**
15. the books you read	**(can change)**
16. the sound made by thunder	**(cannot change)**
17. the color you use to draw a picture	**(can change)**
18. the things in your desk	**(can change)**

19. what time the sun rises   (cannot change)

20. how well you listen   (can change)

21. the day of your birthday   (cannot change)

22. the number of people in your class   (cannot change)

23. how you treat other people   (can change)

24. the day the fair comes to town   (cannot change)

25. how you spend your allowance   (can change)

26. the expression on your face   (can change)

27. how old you are   (cannot change)

28. how fast you eat   (can change)

29. where an elevator stops   (can change)

30. when it rains   (cannot change)

31. the kind of music you listen to   (can change)

32. the colors of the rainbow   (cannot change)

33. the temperature of an oven   (can change)

34. when summer will start   (cannot change)

35. the song robins sing   (cannot change)

36. how strong you are   (can change)

37. what time of day it is   (cannot change)

38. the number of games you know   (can change)

39. how cold it is outside   (cannot change)

40. the loudness of the radio   (can change)

41. when a volcano will erupt   (cannot change)

42. the smell of a rose   (cannot change)

43. how fast you walk   (can change)

44. the depth of the ocean   (cannot change)

45. the length of a pair of pants   (can change)

46. the direction the wind is blowing   (cannot change)

47. the size of a campfire   (can change)

48. how much you weigh   (can change)

49. when the tide comes in or goes out   (cannot change)

50. the number of people you will invite to your birthday
    party   (can change)

51. the shape of an egg   (cannot change)

52. how well you know your math facts   (can change)

53. the kind of plant a seed will grow into   (cannot change)

54. the television programs you watch   (can change)

55. the location of a mountain   (cannot change)

56. the way you treat your friends   (can change)

57. how fast your bicycle goes   (can change)

58. the shape of the moon   (cannot change)

59. the amount of sleep you get at night   (can change)

60. the rotation of the earth   (cannot change)

10   FACT/OPINION

Materials needed
none

☒ total group activity
☒ individual activity
☐ partner activity

Total Group Activity

Read statements from the following list that are either fact or opinion to the students. Use an example such as, "If I said the sun is a star, is that a fact or an opinion?" **(fact—something that is really true or said to be true)**. "What if I said that it's going to rain tomorrow?" **(opinion—a personal belief that is not necessarily true)**. Discuss the answers. Once the students understand the difference between fact and opinion, ask them to stand if they think the statement you read is a fact and remain seated if they think the statement is an opinion.

Variations: Students may respond by putting hands up/hands down, or putting thumbs up/thumbs down. They should sit with their arms folded if they are uncertain.

Remind them to think before responding. To provide ample thinking time, after you read the statement hold up your opened hand and silently count to five. They should respond when you close your fist.

Be certain to ask students to give reasons for their responses. Their answers will often surprise you but will help you to understand their knowledge bases and reasoning processes. In addition, students will usually offer several different reasons for the same answer, which increases the knowledge of all the students.

Adaptation for an Individual Student

Materials needed
lined paper
pencil

The student draws a line down the middle of a piece of paper and labels the two sections "Fact" and "Opinion." In the appropriate column, he or she lists as many statements as possible for each of the categories.

Is It a Fact or an Opinion?

1. Plants need sunshine and water to grow.	**(fact)**
2. John is the nicest person in our class.	**(opinion)**
3. The library is a place to find books.	**(fact)**
4. You can buy things in a store.	**(fact)**
5. It's going to rain tomorrow.	**(opinion)**
6. Earthquakes shake the ground.	**(fact)**
7. Blue is a nice color.	**(opinion)**
8. Deserts are dry places.	**(fact)**
9. Florida is a great place to live.	**(opinion)**
10. Jane always tells lies.	**(opinion)**
11. The heart pumps blood.	**(fact)**

12. *Charlotte's Web* is a good book.   (opinion)

13. Rattlesnakes are poisonous.   (fact)

14. Daisies are pretty flowers.   (opinion)

15. Flour is made from wheat.   (fact)

16. Steel is hard.   (fact)

17. Vanilla ice cream is the best flavor.   (opinion)

18. There are thirty-one days in October.   (fact)

19. Playing hopscotch is more fun than jumping rope.   (opinion)

20. Drums are fun to play.   (opinion)

21. Bees pollinate flowers.   (fact)

22. Dams create lakes.   (fact)

23. When it is daytime here, it is nighttime on the other side of the world.   (fact)

24. California is the best state in the United States.   (opinion)

25. Wheat is a grain.   (fact)

26. Swimming in the ocean is more fun than swimming in a pool.   (opinion)

27. Everyone should get eight hours of sleep.   (opinion)

28. A butterfly is an insect.   (fact)

29. The sun rises in the east.   (fact)

30. Apples make the best pies.   (opinion)

31. Rivers flow from high places to low places.   (fact)

32. Camping is better than staying in a motel.   (opinion)

33. Magnets attract things made out of iron and steel.   (fact)

34. Elizabeth is a nice name for a girl.   (opinion)

35. There are fifty stars on the American flag.   (fact)

36. First grade is more fun than fourth grade.   (opinion)

37. Everyone's fingerprints are different.   (fact)

38. Clouds contain moisture.   (fact)

39. Planes are the best way to travel.   (opinion)

40. The moon travels around the earth.   (fact)

41. It's fun to sing.   (opinion)

42. Lemonade quenches your thirst better than water does.   (opinion)

43. Planes can fly faster than sound.   (fact)

44. Everyone should have a pet.   (opinion)

45. Water can be used to make electricity.   (fact)

46. Hamburgers are better than hotdogs.   (opinion)

47. Mars is a planet.   (fact)

48. Doing science experiments is fun.   (opinion)

49. Dogs make better pets than cats.   (opinion)

50. Mt. Everest is the highest mountain in the world.   (fact)

11 ENCYCLOPEDIA/DICTIONARY

Materials needed
none

☒ total group activity
☒ individual activity
☐ partner activity

Total Group Activity

Review with the students the types of information that can be found in dictionaries and encyclopedias. Remind them that dictionaries are used to determine how a word is spelled and pronounced, what a word means, its proper usage, and its origin. Encyclopedias, on the other hand, are used to locate detailed information about important people, places, and things.

Read students some questions from the following list. They are to decide whether it would be better to look for the information in a dictionary or in an encyclopedia. Read one of the questions, then say aloud, "One ... two ... three ... show me." On the signal "show me," the students should give one of the following hand signals to indicate the category.

Variations: Students may respond by sitting/standing, putting hands up/hands down, or putting thumbs up/thumbs down. If the students look around to see what the others have done before giving their own hand signal, change the directions to "close eyes (pause) show me ... open eyes."

Adaptation for an Individual Student

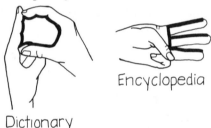

Dictionary

Encyclopedia

Materials needed
lined paper
pencil

The student draws a line down the middle of a piece of paper and labels the two sections "Encyclopedia" and "Dictionary." In the appropriate column, he or she lists as many questions as possible that could be answered by using an encyclopedia or a dictionary.

Is It Found in an Encyclopedia or in a Dictionary?

1. Where does a mudpuppy live? **(encyclopedia)**
2. How do you spell *predicament*? **(dictionary)**
3. Who was the first person to go into space? **(encyclopedia)**
4. What makes a volcano erupt? **(encyclopedia)**
5. How many syllables are in the word *choreography*? **(dictionary)**
6. What did ships look like a long time ago? **(encyclopedia)**
7. How do you pronounce p-o-t p-o-u-r-r-i? **(dictionary)**
8. What is a synonym for the word *aware*? **(dictionary)**
9. What disease is carried by mosquitos? **(encyclopedia)**
10. How many stones were used to build the Great Pyramids? **(encyclopedia)**
11. How do you abbreviate Eastern Standard Time? **(dictionary)**
12. What does a platypus eat? **(encyclopedia)**
13. Does the word *prescription* start with the letters p-r-e or p-e-r? **(dictionary)**
14. What happened during the Great Depression? **(encyclopedia)**

15. Is *backstroke* a compound word or two separate words?   **(dictionary)**

16. When will Halley's Comet be visible from earth?   **(encyclopedia)**

17. How do you hyphenate the word *individual*?   **(dictionary)**

18. How do you spell *colonel*?   **(dictionary)**

19. Who signed the Declaration of Independence?   **(encyclopedia)**

20. Where is the accent in *authenticity*?   **(dictionary)**

21. Why is Marco Polo famous?   **(encyclopedia)**

22. How many syllables are in the word *argumentative*?   **(dictionary)**

23. What is a *tapestry* and what does it look like?   **(encyclopedia)**

24. How does a printing press work?   **(encyclopedia)**

25. What is an antonym for *reject*?   **(dictionary)**

26. How do birds protect themselves?   **(encyclopedia)**

27. How do you pronounce q-u-a-y?   **(dictionary)**

28. What part of speech is the word *desperate*?   **(dictionary)**

29. Are there any differences in color between wild canaries and tame
    canaries?   **(encyclopedia)**

30. Where does the word *amphitheater* come from?   **(dictionary)**

31. What do the stone carvings on Easter Island look like?   **(encyclopedia)**

32. What does the word *corroborate* mean?   **(dictionary)**

33. How does the stock exchange work?   **(encyclopedia)**

34. What happens during an eclipse of the sun?   **(encyclopedia)**

35. Is *receive* spelled r-e-c-i-e-v-e or r-e-c-e-i-v-e?   **(dictionary)**

36. Who invented the telegraph?   **(encyclopedia)**

37. Is the word *groundhog* a compound word or two separate words?   **(dictionary)**

38. How do you hyphenate the word *establishment*?   **(dictionary)**

39. Is Halloween celebrated in other parts of the world?   **(encyclopedia)**

40. When was rabies vaccine first used?   **(encyclopedia)**

41. How do you pronounce g-a-u-c-h-e?   **(dictionary)**

42. How can a person become a citizen of the United States?   **(encyclopedia)**

43. What part of speech is the word *grizzled*?   **(dictionary)**

44. How is thread spun?   **(encyclopedia)**

45. Where does the word *distinguished* come from?   **(dictionary)**

46. How long do elephants live?   **(encyclopedia)**

47. What is a synonym for *assist*?   **(dictionary)**

48. What does a physicist do?   **(encyclopedia)**

49. Which is more acceptable, the word *dived* or the word *dove*?   **(dictionary)**

50. Is the word *bacteria* singular or plural?   **(dictionary)**

51. What happened during the War of 1812?   **(encyclopedia)**

52. What does *dissonance* mean?   **(dictionary)**

53. Where can the midnight sun be seen?   **(encyclopedia)**

54. What do the letters *i.e.* stand for?   **(dictionary)**

55. What is *Esperanto* and how did it originate?   **(encyclopedia)**

56. Is the correct abbreviation for *Thursday*, T-h-u-r. or T-h-u-r-s.? **(dictionary)**

12   SEASONS IN HIDING

Materials needed
none

☒ total group activity
☐ individual activity
☐ partner activity

Total Group Activity

Review the seasons of the year with students. Remind them that the first day of each season begins between the twenty-first and the twenty-third of December, March, June, and September. You may want to put the following on the chalkboard to be used as a reference.

Winter:	December, January, February
Spring:	March, April, May
Summer:	June, July, August
Fall:	September, October, November

Read the following list of comments that students might hear during the different seasons of the year. They are to try to identify the season. Randomly call on students to give answers. After each response you may want to have the other students raise their hands to indicate whether they agree or disagree.

Variation: You can increase the difficulty of this activity by having the students also tell the season that *precedes* or *follows* the one described.

When Would You Hear This?

1. Did you see the beautiful pink blossoms on the tree next door?   **(spring)**
2. It's been so hot that we've gone swimming almost every day!   **(summer)**
3. I love to walk through the leaves and hear them crunch under my feet.   **(fall)**
4. We're all going to Grandma's house for Thanksgiving dinner.   **(fall)**
5. We should plant our vegetable garden this weekend.   **(spring)**
6. Did you see the birds building a nest in our apple tree?   **(spring)**
7. Everything looks like it's covered with a blanket of white.   **(winter)**
8. Oh boy! Tomorrow is Christmas!   **(winter)**
9. The entire hill is covered with wildflowers!   **(spring)**
10. Mom, I'm bored. When will school start?   **(summer)**
11. This March wind is great for flying kites.   **(spring)**
12. I haven't seen the toad in our yard for a while. He must be hibernating.   **(winter)**
13. Did you stay up to watch the fireworks last night?   **(summer)**
14. That's the funniest snowman I've ever seen!   **(winter)**
15. Let's go trick or treating as soon as it gets dark.   **(fall)**
16. Are you going ice skating at the pond after school?   **(winter)**
17. Last night was the first frost of the year.   **(fall)**
18. This morning I saw some little leaves on the tree in the backyard.   **(spring)**
19. That's the lowest I've ever seen the thermometer!   **(winter)**

20. The ducks are starting to leave the lake and migrate south.   **(fall)**

21. It's so hot. Let's go on a picnic.   **(summer)**

22. The fields are all plowed and ready to be planted.   **(spring)**

23. School starts tomorrow!   **(fall)**

24. It seems like every animal we see has a new baby.   **(spring)**

25. The squirrels sure are busy hiding nuts.   **(fall)**

26. Are you going to have a New Year's Eve party?   **(winter)**

27. The temperatures are certainly starting to get cooler.   **(fall)**

28. Yesterday was the hottest day on record.   **(summer)**

29. All the trees look so bare.   **(winter)**

30. I think it's time to put my heavy coat away.   **(spring)**

31. There must have been a thousand people at the beach yesterday!   **(summer)**

32. I love it when the days are so nice and long.   **(summer)**

33. We should go shopping tomorrow and get the things you'll need for the start
    of school.   **(fall)**

34. I think we'll need chains for the car today.   **(winter)**

35. Please pick some tomatoes out of the garden for me.   **(summer)**

36. The daffodils look so pretty out front.   **(spring)**

37. Last night was the longest night of the year.   **(winter)**

38. Let's go to the swimming pool first thing tomorrow morning.   **(summer)**

39. Are you going skiing in the mountains this weekend?   **(winter)**

40. I don't think I've ever seen so many flowers on the rosebush.   **(summer)**

13 BRAINSTORMING: QUESTIONS WITH MULTIPLE ANSWERS

Materials needed
none

☒ total group activity
☒ individual activity
☐ partner activity

Total Group Activity

Read each of the following questions and have students think of as many logical answers as possible. While sample answers are provided, make certain they understand that there is *no one right answer* to any of the questions. Encourage a variety of responses by showing students that you are truly amazed at the diversity of their thinking. You will find that as their confidence grows, this will become one of their favorite activities.

Adaptation for an Individual Student (Grades 5–6)

Materials needed
lined paper
pencil

The student writes as many questions as possible that have multiple answers. These can be used at a later time as a challenge for the whole class.

Brainstorming Questions

1. "It's important you don't lose these," said Kenny to Carl as they left on a week's backpacking trip. What might Kenny have handed Carl? (**matches; map; food...**)

2. "It seems like fall is here," said Jimmy one day as he was walking to school with his friend Jake. What do you think he had in mind when he made this comment? (**leaves changing color; cooler weather; lower angle of the sun for that time of day...**)

3. If your house were on fire, and your family members and pets were on the way out the door, and you had time to grab only one thing, what would it be? (**Answers will vary.**)

4. "There must be an accident on the highway," said Mrs. West. What might have caused her to say this? (**traffic backed up; police car just sped by; flashing red lights ahead...**)

5. How would you know someone had had a fire in a fireplace if you hadn't been there at the time? (**fireplace still warm; wood pile lower; things that were in the fireplace to be burned are no longer there...**)

6. "They're going to build a new highway here," said Dad to Bill as they were driving along. What do you think made Dad say this? (**saw trucks and equipment along the road; saw surveyors; saw stakes marking the path of the highway...**)

7. In a hardware store nails are usually sorted and kept together according to their size. What other things are usually sorted in some way and then kept together? (**books in a library; clothes in a drawer or closet; food in a grocery store...**)

8. How are a chicken and a cow alike? (**both are animals; both give a product that humans use; both are farm animals...**) How are they different? (**two legs/four legs; bird/mammal; one gives eggs/the other gives milk...**)

9. You need a key to start a car. What other uses are there for keys? **(trunks; music boxes; diaries...)**

10. What things do you think are scary to young children? **(darkness; strange sounds; bad dreams...)** What things are scary to children your age? **(Answers will vary.)**

11. How many things can you think of that you've learned by someone teaching you or by actually doing it yourself? **(riding a bike; roller-skating; swimming...)**

12. "No one has lived in that house for a long time," said Daniel, as he and his dad were driving down a country road. What could have made him say this? **(saw broken windows; saw grass and weeds overgrown; saw boards falling off the house...)**

13. "I see you had a cup of hot chocolate before going to bed last night," said Mother to Kristin one morning. But mother hadn't seen Kristin drink the hot chocolate. How might she have known this? **(saw cup with dried hot chocolate inside; saw empty package of instant hot chocolate mix; saw where she had spilled some hot chocolate...)**

14. How might you know an animal was frightened or angry? **(heard growl; saw hunched back; saw it run or hide...)**

15. How can you tell when a friend is mad at you? **(won't talk to you; won't look at you; looks at you with an angry expression...)**

16. If you were digging at the beach and hit something hard, what might it be? **(a rock; a bottle; a box...)**

17. If you came out of a large store and realized you were lost, what could you do? **(ask someone for help; go back in the store and tell one of the salesclerks your problem; ask where the nearest telephone is and call home...)**

18. What situations make adults really mad? **(telling lies; losing something; messy rooms...)** What makes children really mad? **(when someone won't play with them; when someone cheats in a game; when they're punished and miss out on something they really wanted to do...)**

19. What sounds could you recognize *without* seeing what made the noise? **(a cat's meow; the honk of a car's horn; a ring of the telephone...)**

20. How might you know someone has been injured? **(saw the person limping; saw people standing around the person; saw an ambulance arrive...)**

21. If you were principal of a school, what might cause you to close your school for twenty-four hours? **(flood; holiday; fire...)**

22. How might you find out that there was going to be a circus in town? **(see trucks or trains arrive with the animals; see billboards or flyers; hear it advertised on radio or television...)**

23. Some words name numbers: three, ten, twenty, etc. Other words do not directly tell you a number, but when you hear them you often think of a number. For instance, week and the number seven seem to go together. What other words make you think of numbers? **(duet—two; weekend—two; triangle—three; dozen—twelve; century—one hundred; shutout—zero...)**

24. If a new city were going to be built, what types of buildings would be needed? **(library; police station; grocery store...)**

25. "What did you paint today?" Dad asked Sherrie. How could Dad have known that Sherrie painted something? **(saw paint on her clothes; smelled paint or turpentine; noticed the paint can had not been put away...)**

26. Sharks and whales are similar in many ways. For instance, both swim and both live in the ocean. In what ways are they different? **(fish/mammal; size; color...)**

27. We use our hands every day to do many different things. What are some ways that people use their hands? **(to button or zip clothes; to pick things up; to wave at people...)**

28. Plant seeds are found in unusual places. How could they have gotten to these places? **(blown by the wind; buried by an animal; carried in the fur of an animal...)**

29. What could you find out by looking at an airplane schedule? **(where they go; how often they fly to certain cities; what time of day they leave and arrive...)**

30. While taking a trip Barbara said, "This would certainly *not* be a good place to grow crops." What might have caused her to say this? **(rocky land; cold weather; lack of water...)**

31. What tasks can you think of that used to be done by hand, but are now done by machines? **(washing clothes; sweeping floors or rugs; cutting lumber...)**

32. If you lost your dog, how might you go about trying to find it? **(talk to neighbors; put signs up in the neighborhood; walk around the neighborhood calling the dog's name...)**

33. How can you tell if a person is very strong? **(ask the person to lift something heavy; look at his or her muscles; observe the body build...)**

34. Why are all homes or shelters throughout the world *not* alike? **(climate; function; materials available...)**

35. Animals do not all have the same number of legs. In fact, some do not have legs at all. What animals can you name that do not have legs? **(whale; worm; slug; coral...)** Which animals have two legs? **(pigeon; parakeet; ostrich...)** Which animals have four legs? **(deer; frog; lizard...)** Insects have six legs. Can you name some insects? **(wasp; ladybug; grasshopper; ant...)** What animals have eight legs? **(octopus; tarantula; scorpion...)**

36. As Frank and his parents drove into the city, his father said, "We're lucky we didn't get here a half hour ago." Why might his father have made this comment? **(heard on the radio that there had been an accident; saw traffic was backed up and just starting to clear; just missed rush hour traffic...)**

37. How might you know it was windy outside, even though you were indoors? **(saw leaves on trees moving; saw people's clothing blowing; saw leaves or paper blowing along the ground...)**

38. "There must have just been a wedding," said Kathy to her friend Julie. What might have caused her to say this? **(saw a car decorated; saw rice on the ground; saw people standing outside the church waiting for the bride and groom to come out...)**

39. If a great scientist were going to start working on a new invention, and he asked you what invention you thought would be most useful for the world today, what would you say? **(Answers will vary.)**

40. If there were a deep hole in the ground, how could you tell how deep it was? **(tie a rock on a string and lower it, then measure the string; yell down and listen to the echo; throw a stone in the hole and listen for it to hit bottom...)**

41. If you were in charge of changing the school lunches, but you had to continue to provide balanced meals, what changes would you make? **(Answers will vary.)**

42. Collecting stamps is one kind of hobby. What other hobbies can you name? **(collecting coins; collecting bottle caps; photography...)**

43. What makes a good teacher? **(makes learning interesting; is patient; explains things clearly...)**

44. If you were camping in the woods and saw what looked like lights through the trees, what might they be? **(people with flashlights; eyes of an animal; campfires...)**

45. How is a human being like a machine? **(both need energy in order to keep working; both have moving parts; both can do work...)** How are they different? **(the human breathes; the machine is made of metal; the person can think...)**

46. How can someone your age earn money? **(Answers will vary depending on the age of the students.)**

47. "Just think how easy it is to drive all the way across the country now," said Alice. "I'm sure glad I didn't have to make the trip in the days of the covered wagon." What are some differences Alice might have been thinking about? **(quality of roads; dangers; places to sleep and eat...)**

48. If a new student who spoke no English joined your class, what could you do to make him or her feel at home? (**show the student how to play different recess games; teach the student some English words and find out how to say the same word in his or her language; show the student around the classroom and around the school...**)

49. A caterpillar changes and becomes a butterfly or moth. What are some other things that change with time? (**people; animals; mountains...**)

50. About 70 percent of the earth is covered with water. That leaves 30 percent that is land. But we do not live on all of the land. Why not? (**too dry; too cold; too hot; too mountainous...**)

51. The *foot* of a mountain is one use of the word *foot*. How else is the word *foot (feet)* used? (**foot of a table; foot of a chair; foot of a river; feet per second...**)

52. What things can you think of that come in twos? (**hands; headlights on cars; twins...**) In threes? (**triplets; wheels on a tricycle; points on a triangle...**) In fours? (**sides of a square; legs on a chair; bases in baseball...**) In fives? (**fingers; points on a star; quintuplets...**)

53. "These trees are very old," said Bev. How might she have known this? (**height of trees; circumference of trees; gnarled trunks on trees...**)

54. In what ways are plants and animals alike? (**both are living; both reproduce; both need water and nutrients...**)

55. How many different ways can you think of to group the numbers zero to twenty-five? (**odd or even; according to the number of digits; numbers that are made of straight lines only...**)

56. A hairpin is one use of the word *pin*. How else is the word *pin* used? (**bobby pin; straight pin; jewelry pin; rolling pin...**)

57. What inventions from the past are most useful to us today? (**Answers will vary.**)

58. How are a computer and a typewriter alike? (**both have a keyboard; both can be used for writing; people type on both of them...**)

59. If you say a person is *determined*, that indicates how the person feels. How many other ways can you name that describe how a person feels? (**selfish; confused; nervous; angry...**)

60. How many books can you think of in which the animals talk like people? (**The Cat in the Hat; Charlotte's Web; Alice in Wonderland; Just So Stories; Winnie the Pooh...**)

14   TWENTY QUESTIONS

Materials needed

Total Group Activity

One student or group of students is sent from the room. The others choose an object. The student or group of students returns to the room and asks up to twenty questions that can be answered with "yes", "no", "partly", or "I don't know", to find out what object was chosen.

To narrow the choice, encourage students to ask broad questions first such as, "Is it an animal?" "Is it in existence now?" "Is it larger than a house?" and so on. As the clues mount, more specific questions will prove helpful. The students continue questioning either until the object is guessed or until twenty questions have been asked. After twenty questions have been asked, the person or each person in the group may make one final guess.

Variations: The level of difficulty of this activity can easily be adjusted to correspond with the age and ability levels of your students. For young children specify that the object must be something that is visible within the room. Or you can name a category from which the object must be chosen, such as animals, things you eat, and so on. Older students will enjoy playing the game with animal, vegetable, and mineral categories. In this context, *animal* refers to any living thing that can eat, move, or produce young, and includes anything from products of animals. *Vegetables* include things that grow in the ground and anything made from plants or plant products. Items that do not fit into the animal or vegetable groups are classified as *mineral*.

15   UNKNOWN OBJECT

Materials needed
small box
an object that will fit into the box

☒ total group activity
☐ individual activity
☐ partner activity

Total Group Activity

Secretly place an object, such as a pencil, piece of chalk, or pair of scissors, in a small box. Show the box to the students and tell them there is something inside of it. They are to try to discover its identity by asking questions that you can answer with "yes", "no", or "partly". The students continue questioning until the object is guessed. Confirm their guesses by unveiling the "mystery object."

Variation: An alternate version of this game involves establishing the rule that no one may ask a question using the name of the object, i.e., "Is it a pencil?" If someone does, say, "Sorry, I can't answer that." Have students continue to ask questions that give hints about the object until it seems that almost everyone has discovered the identity of the object. Then tell them that if they have listened carefully to the clues, they should know what is in the box, but they should *not* reveal the object. Descriptive questions may still be asked by the whole class until everyone knows what is in the box. This may sound frustrating, but students love this version and become very involved. Besides, you'll be amazed to see how intently they listen when they know the answer will not be given!

16   OBJECTS WITH BODY PARTS

Materials needed
none

☒ total group activity
☒ individual activity
☐ partner activity

Total Group Activity

Explain to students that some objects have parts with names that are the same as names of parts of our bodies. For instance, we have a head and a nail has a head. Then ask what body part or parts each of the items in the following list have.

LOOK AT MY EYE!

HEY! YOU MAY HAVE AN EYE, BUT IT SURE ISN'T LIKE MINE!

Adaptation for an Individual Student

Materials needed
lined paper
pencil

The student lists as many objects as he or she can think of that have the same names as human body parts.

What Body Part Does This Have?

1. clock	**(face, hands)**		14. dress	**(neck, waist, shoulders)**
2. needle	**(eye)**		15. bed	**(foot, head)**
3. shirt	**(neck)**		16. cornstalk	**(ears)**
4. pin	**(head)**		17. saw	**(teeth)**
5. glove	**(wrist, palm, fingers)**		18. river	**(mouth)**
6. bottle	**(neck)**		19. loaf of bread	**(heels)**
7. potato	**(eyes, skin)**		20. sewing machine	**(head)**
8. jar	**(mouth)**		21. trousers	**(legs, waist)**
9. zipper	**(teeth)**		22. sprinkler	**(head)**
10. shoe	**(tongue, eyes, toe, heel)**		23. storm	**(eye)**
11. car	**(body)**		24. macaroni	**(elbows)**
12. chair	**(legs, arms, back, seat, feet)**		25. road	**(shoulders)**
13. socks	**(heel, toe)**			

17   HOW ARE THESE ALIKE?

Materials needed

Total Group Activity

Ask students how the following pairs of items are alike. Encourage them to think beyond the items' obvious similarities and to look for interrelationships that may never have occurred to them before.

How Are These Alike?

1. sweater/blanket   (both used for warmth; both used by people; both used as a cover...)

2. puppy/baby   (both are offspring; both are wiggly; both cry or whimper when they are unhappy...)

3. rain/tears   (both are transparent; both trickle or run; both associated with sadness...)

4. scissors/lawn mower   (both have blades; both must move in order to work; both are used by people...)

5. newspaper/book   (both convey thoughts/knowledge; both use words as written symbols; both are printed...)

6. barn/motel   (both provide shelter; both have similar shapes; both have inhabitants...)

7. saw/comb   (both have teeth; both have pointed edges; both are held in people's hands...)

8. wind/water   (both can be used as energy sources; both can be destructive; both can move objects...)

9. volcano/fireworks   (both can be dangerous; both can be spectacular to watch; both shoot out sparks...)

10. fish/soap   (both can float; both go in water; both are slippery when wet...)

11. ice skates/stilts   (a person can easily fall when learning to use both of them; both become appendages of people; both are used for recreation...)

12. candle/pencil   (both have elongated shapes; both have an interior part which differs from the outside; both get shorter with use...)

13. dragon/volcano   (both shoot sparks; both create fear and fascination; both could be dangerous or destructive...)

14. kite/sailboat   (both are moved by wind; both are used for recreation; both sail...)

15. jet/bird   (both fly; both have wings; both utilize air currents...)

16. river/rainstorm   (both move; both can be destructive; both can be helpful...)

17. bread/oatmeal   (both are grains; both are eaten for breakfast; both are cooked...)

18. Fall/old age   (both are part of a cycle; both are symbols of approaching the end of life; both can be a time of slowing down and peace...)

19. eagle/lion   (both are symbols of power; both are predators; both have been hunted by man...)

20. hairpin/rolling pin   (both have elongated shapes; both are used for controlling a material; both are man-made...)

18   ANALOGIES

Materials needed

[X]   total group activity
[X]   individual activity
[ ]   partner activity

Total Group Activity

Analogies are often baffling to children because they do not have a systematic way to approach solving them. For instance, you may present the analogy:

Cow is to milk as
chicken is to ———————,

and a child may answer "feed." The student has established a relationship, but not the correct one.

The following approach guides children through the necessary thinking steps. Once students understand how to work analogies they become successful and very excited about them. This invariably results in analogies becoming one of their favorite language arts thinking activities.

Procedure: Explain to students that they are going to play a game using words that go together. Say a pair of words and then say the first word of a second pair. They are to act as detectives and try to find the missing word.

Explain that the "clue" is to discover why and how the first pair go together.

Give the example:

Goose is to gosling as
cow is to ———————.

Ask what makes goose and gosling go together. When it's determined that a gosling is a baby goose, explain that the way to complete the second pair is to ask yourself, "If a gosling is called a baby goose, then what is a baby cow called?"

Read the first word pair of another analogy:

Water is to swim

Ask how these words go together. When they determine that you swim in water, give them the second pair:

Water is to swim as
ice is to ———————. **(skate)**

Once the correct answer has been given, summarize the thinking process:

"You swim in water.
Ask yourself, 'What do you do on ice?'—Skate.
Therefore, water is to swim as
ice is to skate."

Continue in this manner, guiding them through several analogies, each time having them clarify the relationship of the first words before attempting to complete the analogy.

When they are confident of the procedure, read an analogy, omitting the final word. Each time a student gives a correct answer, acknowledge that it is correct. Then have the student explain how the first words were related and how this led to the answer. This continuously reinforces the process for those children who are less secure.

If an incorrect answer is given, help the child go back through the thinking process: "How do the first words go together?" and so on.

In the following analogies, one answer is given in parentheses. However, any answer that maintains a logical relationship should be accepted.

Adaptation for an Individual Student

Materials needed
unlined paper (6″ x 9″ for class book)
pencil

    The student writes as many analogies as he or she can think of. These can later be used as a challenge for the whole class. Or the student can write each analogy on a separate piece of 6″ x 9″ paper, omitting the answer on the front and writing it with an illustration, if desired, on the reverse side.

    When a sufficient number of these papers has been collected, they can be assembled in a thought-provoking class puzzle book.

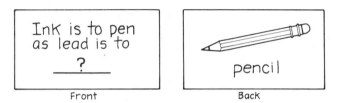

Front   Back

Analogies

1. Duck is to waddle as frog is to _____ **(hop).**
2. Shower is to bathroom as dishwasher is to _____ **(kitchen).**
3. Baseball is to throw as soccer ball is to _____ **(kick).**
4. Plumber is to pipe wrench as carpenter is to _____ **(hammer).**
5. Ink is to pen as lead is to _____ **(pencil).**
6. Chickens are to grain as cattle are to _____ **(grass).**
7. Curtains are to windows as sunglasses are to _____ **(eyes).**
8. Potato is to vegetable as grape is to _____ **(fruit).**
9. Red is to stop as yellow is to _____ **(caution).**
10. Boat is to water as plane is to _____ **(air).**
11. Rain is to warm weather as snow is to _____ **(cold weather).**
12. Blackberries are to bushes as oranges are to _____ **(trees).**
13. Man is to boy as woman is to _____ **(girl).**
14. Grass is to green as sky is to _____ **(blue).**
15. Water is to wet as desert is to _____ **(dry).**
16. Perfume is to nose as music is to _____ **(ears).**
17. Fish is to swim as human is to _____ **(walk).**
18. Table is to dining room as bed is to _____ **(bedroom).**
19. Hotdog is to eat as milk is to _____ **(drink).**
20. Dentist is to office as salesperson is to _____ **(store).**
21. Ice cube is to glass as wood is to _____ **(fireplace).**
22. Steaks are to cattle as pork chops are to _____ **(pigs).**
23. Apple is to skin as nut is to _____ **(shell).**
24. Ping-Pong is to paddle as tennis is to _____ **(racket).**
25. Foot is to big toe as hand is to _____ **(thumb).**
26. Duck is to quack as hen is to _____ **(cluck).**

27. Firecracker is to the Fourth of July as jack-o'lantern is to _____ (**Halloween**).

28. Cool is to cold as warm is to _____ (**hot**).

29. Smell is to nose as touch is to _____ (**fingers**).

30. Freddy is to boy as Sally is to _____ (**girl**).

31. Crayon is to coloring as brush is to _____ (**painting**).

32. Teacher is to students as coach is to _____ (**players**).

33. Food is to mouth as thread is to _____ (**needle**).

34. Sausage is to pork as hamburger is to _____ (**beef**).

35. Hood is to car as hat is to _____ (**head**).

36. Collie is to dog as pigeon is to _____ (**bird**).

37. Flour is to wheat as sawdust is to _____ (**wood**).

38. Laugh is to hyena as hoot is to _____ (**owl**).

39. Seaweed is to ocean as cactus is to _____ (**desert**).

40. Pencil is to write as needle is to _____ (**sew**).

41. Mailcarrier is to letters as librarian is to _____ (**books**).

42. Crops are to farm as fruit is to _____ (**orchard**).

43. Body is to clothes as banana is to _____ (**peel**).

44. Roof is to house as steeple is to _____ (**church**).

45. Forest is to trees as lake is to _____ (**water**).

46. Wolf is to howl as sparrow is to _____ (**chirp**).

47. City is to people as farm is to _____ (**animals**).

48. End is to beginning as stop is to _____ (**go**).

49. Boat is to sail as plane is to _____ (**fly**).

50. Lawyer is to court as teacher is to _____ (**classroom**).

51. Catch is to throw as push is to _____ (**pull**).

52. Grass is to dirt as blacktop is to _____ (**road**).

53. Monkey is to tree as hippopotamus is to _____ (**water**).

54. City is to buildings as crowd is to _____ (**people**).

55. Bean is to vine as corn is to _____ (**stalk**).

56. Table lamp is to house as lamppost is to _____ (**street**).

57. Rabbit is to fur as porcupine is to _____ (**quills**).

58. Tree is to tall as bush is to _____ (**short**).

59. Bear is to forest as monkey is to _____ (**jungle**).

60. Sunrise is to dawn as sunset is to _____ (**evening**).

61. Florist is to flowers as farmer is to _____ (**crops**).

62. Lamp is to bulb as socket is to _____ (**plug**).

63. Tailor is to cloth as butcher is to _____ (**meat**).

64. Skin is to humans as scales are to _____ (**fish**).

65. Noise is to loud as whisper is to _____ (**soft**).

66. Ankle is to foot as wrist is to _____ (**arm**).

67. Motel is to lodging as restaurant is to _____ (**food**).

68. Alley is to narrow as street is to _____ (**wide**).

69. Heavy is to light as large is to _____ (**small**).

70. Grapes are to vineyards as pineapples are to _____ (**plantations**).

19   HERE'S THE ANSWER—WHAT WAS THE QUESTION?

Materials needed
none

☒   total group activity
☒   individual activity
☐   partner activity

Total Group Activity

This activity is the opposite of what usually happens in the classroom. Explain to students that you will give them the *answer* to a question, and that they are to think of the questions that might have resulted in this answer. For each of the answers you read, there will be several possible questions that could have been asked. Sample questions are provided here. For example, if the answer is "the Dodgers," the questions might have been:
—Who won the game?
—What's your favorite baseball team?
—What is the name of a major league baseball team in Los Angeles?
Give several examples before starting this activity so students get used to thinking "in reverse."

Adaptation for an Individual Student

Materials needed
lined paper
pencil

The student writes as many statements as possible that could be the answers to a variety of questions. He or she also lists the questions that might have been asked. These can be used at a later time as a challenge for the whole class.

Here's the Answer—What Was the Question?

1. Let's go investigate!

(**I wonder what that noise was? What's that smell? I wonder why our dog is whimpering?...**)

2. under the bed

(**Where are your shoes? Where did that sound come from? Where did the cat hide?...**)

3. in the morning

(**When do you have breakfast? When do you go to school? When do the birds start to sing?...**)

4. Hawaii

(**What state grows the most pineapples? What state has the most active volcanoes? Where did you go on your vacation?...**)

5. in a lake

(**Where do you sail your boat? Where do you like to water-ski? Where do you go swimming?...**)

6. a barking dog

(**What awakened you? What scared the burglar? What made the people think that there might be a fire in the house?...**)

7. fish

(**What could you catch in a river? What's swimming in that bowl? What did you eat for dinner last night?...**)

8. noon

(When do you eat lunch? What is the middle of the day called? What's another name for 12:00 PM? . . .)

9. in a minute

(When will we be leaving? When is the bell going to ring? When will you be ready? . . .)

10. my dad

(Who taught you to play ball? Who brought you to school today? Who cooked dinner? . . .)

11. in the park

(Where did you fall down? Where did you find that dollar? Where did you play marbles? . . .)

12. under the ground

(Where do you find worms? Where are the roots of trees? Where does a gopher live? . . .)

13. in the middle

(Where are you in this picture? Where is the dividing line painted on the freeway? Where should you cut the cake in order to divide it in half? . . .)

14. beside the house

(Where did you park your bike? Where is the garbage can? Where did you find the newspaper? . . .)

15. the fence

(What did he climb over? What did he hit the ball over? What did the plants climb up? . . .)

16. a good friend

(What would you hate to lose? Who would help you if you had a problem? Who would you like to have spend the night? . . .)

17. a jet

(What's that up in the sky? What made that roaring sound? What can quickly take you to a faraway place? . . .)

18. when it rains

(When is a good time to stay indoors? When do you open your umbrella? When do you use windshield wipers? . . .)

19. in the library

(Where should you be quiet? Where did you find that book? Where would you find books, newspapers, magazines, and encyclopedias? . . .)

20. Yes!

(Would you like to go to the movies with me? Would you like an ice cream cone? Would you like to take a vacation? . . .)

21. bones

(What is a skeleton made of? What do dogs like to chew on? What part of a fish do you not want to eat? . . .)

22. water

(What was ice before it was frozen? What is in a river? What do you you drink when you're thirsty? . . .)

23. They swim.

(What do fish do? What do people do when they fall in water? What do ducks do in a pond? . . .)

24. at the circus

(Where did you see the lions? Where did you get the balloon? Where were the clowns? . . .)

25. a mouse

(What made him scream? What runs around the house at night? What would a cat like to catch? . . .)

20   IDIOMS

Materials needed
none

☒ total group activity
☒ individual activity
☐ partner activity

Total Group Activity

Idioms are always amusing to students. Explain that their meanings are quite different when they are taken literally. For instance, when talking about baseball, if you say that someone stole a base, you most certainly don't mean that the person sneaked in and took one of the bases. Yet that is what the words indicate. You might mention how difficult it is for people who are learning a new language to understand idioms, since they read each of the words and interpret the meanings literally.

Read the following list of idioms and have the students explain the intended and literal meanings of each.

Adaptation for an Individual Student

Materials needed
unlined paper (8½″ x 11″ for class book)
pencil

The student copies one of the following idioms on a piece of paper (8½″ x 11″ for class usage). He or she then illustrates the literal meaning of the idiom. A collection of these can later be assembled into a delightful class book.

Follow-Up Activity: Individual students may research the expressions to find out where they came from. *Brewer's Dictionary of Phrase and Fable,* by E. Cobham Brewer (New York: Harper & Row, 1981), is an excellent resource.

What Does This Mean?

1. Don't make a mountain out of a molehill.
2. It's time to hit the road.
3. I've got it right on the tip of my tongue.
4. You hit the nail on the head.
5. You've left me in the dark.
6. It's been raining cats and dogs all day.
7. I've got butterflies in my stomach.
8. Did you see him blow his top?
9. His bark is worse than his bite.
10. A bird in the hand is worth two in the bush.
11. She's got bats in her belfry.
12. He's as sharp as a tack.
13. Don't count your chickens before they hatch.
14. He's a real turkey.
15. I think he's got something up his sleeve.
16. He jumped out of the frying pan and into the fire.
17. I'm all thumbs today.
18. You really have a green thumb.
19. That sounds like it's up my alley.
20. I wish he'd go fly a kite.
21. I think we'd better throw in the towel.
22. I'm afraid we bought a lemon.
23. Don't get upset. She's just pulling your leg.
24. He's a real eager beaver.
25. She was born with a silver spoon in her mouth.
26. Don't be a stick in the mud.
27. There he goes crying wolf again.
28. Let's turn the tables on them.
29. Now you're cooking with gas.
30. That's like the pot calling the kettle black.

21 YELLOW PAGES QUIZ

Materials needed
none

☒ total group activity
☒ individual activity
☐ partner activity

Total Group Activity

Review the topical organization of the telephone book's Yellow Pages with the class. Explain that sometimes when they look for information under a particular topic, the book will direct them to a different heading. However, other times there will be no listing at all under the first topic that occurs to them. In this case they need to think of alternate names for the same information and look them up.

Read the following list of situations that might necessitate using the Yellow Pages. The students' job is to try to determine under which heading the information would be listed. While sample answers from actual Yellow Pages are provided here, Yellow Pages' headings may vary for your area. Students should brainstorm possible answers, not necessarily the actual headings.

Adaptation for an Individual Student

Materials needed
lined paper
pencil

The student writes as many situations as he or she can think of that would require using the Yellow pages of the telephone book to locate needed information. Have the student also write the headings under which the information would be listed. These can be used at a later time as a challenge for the whole class.

Under Which Heading in the Yellow Pages Would You Look for This?

1. You'd like to build a model train layout. (**Hobby and Model Construction Supplies**)
2. You wonder how much a sports trophy costs. (**Trophies**)
3. You need to take your pet to an animal hospital. (**Veterinarians**)
4. You want to find out who teaches ballet classes. (**Dancing Instruction**)
5. You'd like to buy a book. (**Book Dealers—Retail**)
6. You want to train your dog. (**Dog and Pet Training**)
7. You'd like to purchase a program for your computer. (**Computers—Software and Services**)
8. Your mom says you may order some Chinese food to bring home for dinner. (**Foods—Carryout**)
9. You want to find out how much clarinet lessons would cost. (**Music Instruction—Instrumental**)
10. You have a collection of comic books and want to know the value of one unusual one. (**Book Dealers—Used and Rare**)
11. You'd like to buy oil paints, brushes, and a canvas. (**Artists' Materials and Supplies**)
12. You want to buy a used camera. (**Photographic Equipment and Supplies—Retail**)
13. Your dad has locked his keys in the car. (**Locks and Locksmiths**)
14. You decide to make a birdhouse and need some wood. (**Lumber—Retail**)

15. You want to buy a plant for the yard for your dad's birthday. (**Nurseries—Plants, Trees**)

16. You'd like to find out how much judo lessons cost. (**Karate and Other Martial Arts Instruction**)

17. You need to get new eyeglasses. (**Optometrists—Doctors of Optometry**)

18. You're going away on vacation and need a place that will take care of your kitten. (**Kennels**)

19. You want to buy a new tennis racket. (**Sporting Goods—Retail**)

20. Your parents need someone to fix their car. (**Automobile Repair and Service**)

21. You'd like to start a stamp collection and want to know where you can buy stamps. (**Stamps for Collectors**)

22. You need to know what time the movie at the theater starts. (**Theaters**)

23. You want to go horseback riding. (**Stables**)

24. Your parents would like to buy wood for the fireplace. (**Firewood**)

25. You'd like to find out how much a hamster costs. (**Pet Shops**)

22   KEY WORD CONNECTIONS

Materials needed
none

☒ total group activity
☒ individual activity
☐ partner activity

Total Group Activity

Ask how many students have tried to look up something in an encyclopedia and have not been able to find it. Explain that it is often necessary to think about other headings where the information might be found in order to be successful.

Ask the students to try to determine where information about the topics on the following list would be located. Stress that it is all right for them to make some wrong guesses. The important thing is for them to think of alternative headings so that the information can be found eventually. While sample answers are provided here, they are not the only ones possible.* Headings will vary among encyclopedias.

Adaptation for an Individual Student

Materials needed
lined paper
pencil

The student writes as many topics as he or she can think of which might necessitate using an encyclopedia to locate information. The topic under which the information would be listed should also be written. These can be used at a later time as a challenge for the whole class.

Under Which Heading in the Encyclopedia Would You Look for This?

1. what prehistoric man ate   **(Food)**
2. sizes of birds' eggs   **(Bird)**
3. Tomb of the Unknown Soldier   **(Unknown Soldier)**
4. collecting and displaying shells   **(Shell)**
5. instincts of dogs   **(Dog)**
6. why all homes are not alike   **(Shelter)**
7. how weather balloons are used   **(Weather)**
8. how animals move about   **(Animal)**
9. how scientists study atoms   **(Atom)**
10. superstitions about cats   **(Cat)**
11. Greek and Roman gods   **(Mythology)**

---

*Based on information in *The World Book Encyclopedia* (Chicago: World Book, Inc., 1983).

12. measuring distance in space   **(Astronomy)**
13. frontier towns   **(Western Frontier Life)**
14. animal teeth   **(Teeth)**
15. homes during the Colonial period   **(Shelter)**
16. refuges for birds   **(Bird)**
17. how airplanes have changed the world   **(Aviation)**
18. tribes of American Indians   **(Indian, American)**
19. Greek theater   **(Drama)**
20. brains of animals   **(Brain)**
21. silkworms   **(Moth)**
22. how early Americans dressed   **(Colonial Life in America)**
23. natural resources of America   **(United States)**
24. the size of the ice cap   **(Antarctica)**
25. basic food groups   **(Nutrition)**

23 WHAT-WOULD-YOU-DO? STORIES

Materials needed
none

☒ total group activity
☐ individual activity
☐ partner activity

Total Group Activity

Read each of the following stories and then ask the students what they think the person might do. Encourage a variety of solutions and discussion about the possible consequences of each solution.

A. MY FRIEND WANTS TO PLAY, BUT MY OTHER FRIENDS SAY NO (Grades 2–6)

In Bradd's backyard there was a huge oak tree. Whenever Bradd and his friends Matt and Carl played in the backyard they always talked about how much fun it would be to build a fort in the tree. Bradd asked his dad about it, and he promised that someday when he had a little extra time he'd take Bradd to the lumberyard to get wood and they would build the fort together.

During summer vacation Matt and Carl went to their grandmother's for a long visit, and at first Bradd was very lonesome. Then he started playing with Freddy who lived down the block. Freddy had lived in the neighborhood just about as long as Bradd had, but they hadn't played together much. It seemed that Freddy just didn't fit in when Bradd, Matt, and Carl were playing together. And, besides, a lot of times Matt and Carl weren't very nice to Freddy, so he usually went home. But now with Matt and Carl gone, Bradd found himself playing with Freddy almost every day, and, as time went by, the two of them became really good friends.

One Saturday morning Bradd's dad said he had time to build the fort. Bradd dashed out of the house to tell Freddy the good news and they were back in no time, waiting for Dad to get his car keys. All weekend the three of them worked on the fort and by dinnertime Sunday it was finished. There was no doubt in Freddy's and Bradd's minds that it was the best fort anyone had ever built! For the rest of the summer they spent more time in the fort than anywhere else.

Early one morning toward the end of summer vacation, Bradd heard a knock on his door. When he opened it there were Matt and Carl. The first thing Bradd said was, "Oh boy, you're back! Just wait 'til you see what's new in the backyard!" The three boys raced through the house and into the backyard. When Matt and Carl saw the tree fort, they shouted together, "You built the tree fort!" They all climbed the ladder and were having a wonderful time playing in the fort when Freddy arrived. Carl whispered to Bradd, "What's *he* doing here? He's a creep. Tell him to go home."
WHAT COULD BRADD DO?

B. MY FOLKS SAID NOT TO HAVE ANYONE OVER, BUT...(Grades 2–6)

Just like always, Kim walked home from school, poured herself a glass of milk, took some cookies from the cookie jar, and sat down at the kitchen table to think. This was always the loneliest part of the day for her. Her parents wouldn't be home for another three hours and the rule was that she could go to a friend's house, but under no circumstances was she to have anyone play at her house when her parents were gone. And that was the problem. Because both of her parents worked, it was late before they got home. Some of her friends used to invite her over after school, but she never got to ask them to her house. After a while they just stopped asking her to come over and now she was alone—and hating it—until her parents came home.

As she sat at the table thinking, she looked out the window and saw Julie walking down the sidewalk. Kim ran to the door and called, "Hi Julie! What's new?" Then, without pausing, she blurted out, "Mom made some really good cookies last night. Want to come in and have some?" Julie answered, "Sure!" The next thing Kim knew, the two of them were sitting at the kitchen table talking and eating cookies. Then Kim told Julie about the new game she had and they went to her room to look at it. They sat on the bed and talked some more, then started to play the game. Right in the middle of a game, Julie looked at her watch and said, "Oh, look what time it is! I'd better get home or I'll be late for dinner. I'll tell you what. I'll come by after school tomorrow and we can finish the game." Kim replied, "Super! I'll see you then."

As soon as Julie had gone, Kim felt guilty. She knew she wasn't supposed to have anyone over when her parents were gone. But she had had so much fun that afternoon. And oh, how she wanted Julie to come over the next day. She kept thinking about what she should do as she cleared the kitchen table and washed and dried the glasses. Just as she was finishing, she heard her parents drive up. Her mom walked in the door and said, "Hi Kim! How was your day?" Kim answered, "Oh, fine." Then her mom asked, "What did you do after school today?"

WHAT MIGHT KIM SAY?

C. TO PAY OR NOT TO PAY? (Grades 2–6)

Billy had been collecting aluminum cans all year. He hoped that before baseball tryouts he'd have enough money to buy a new glove and bat. He knew it would be important to practice with the glove and bat before he tried out, and everything was working out just right. He still had two weeks left and today was the day he was going to sell his last load of cans.

As soon as Mr. Garland paid him for the cans, Billy counted all his money. Sure enough, he had what he needed plus $1.50 extra! "Boy, that was close!" he thought, "but I've got enough." Off he raced to the sporting goods store to buy the bat and glove he'd been looking at for the last six months. But when he got to the store, he couldn't believe his eyes. The glove had gone up in price! Now he'd have only enough money to buy it alone. The bat would have to wait until he could earn more money. And there was no way he could get enough money before tryouts.

Sadly he walked up to the cash register to pay. The salesperson picked up the glove but didn't even look at the price. To Billy's surprise, he rang up the old amount instead of the new price. Billy thought to himself, "He must have forgotten that the price has gone up." He started to say something, then a thought occurred to him. "If I don't say anything, I'll have enough money to get the bat, too. And I really want that bat." Just then the salesman interrupted his thinking to ask, "Is there anything else you want?"

WHAT MIGHT BILLY DO?

D. EYEWITNESS TO A THEFT, BUT. . .(Grades 3–6)

Steve and Kevin had been friends since first grade. They always walked home from school together, and most afternoons you could find them at the park shooting baskets.

One afternoon as they were leaving school, Kevin saw one of the boys in his class with a basketball. "Hey, Steve!" he said, "Let's stop and shoot some baskets before we go home." Steve replied, "Sure!" and put his books on the ground where they would be out of the way. Some other kids joined in and they all ended up playing a game.

That night after dinner, when Steve got ready to do his homework, he remembered he had forgotten to pick up his books after the basketball game. He decided the best thing to do would be to go back to school in the hope that the books were still there.

As he ran along, all he could think about was that the books he had left on the ground were the library books he needed to use for his science report. He kept thinking, "How will I ever pay for them if someone has taken them? They're all expensive books."

After what seemed like an eternity, he got to school and peered through the shadows at the spot where he had left the books. His heart sank as he realized they weren't where he had left them. He kept walking around searching in the hope that someone might have moved them. Finally he had to admit to himself that they were gone.

As he turned to walk home, he heard voices by the side of the building. "Maybe those kids have seen my books," he thought. He started to run toward the building but saw something that made him stop in amazement. There, climbing through a broken window with the new school T.V. and a tape recorder, were Kevin and another boy. Steve simply couldn't believe his eyes.

Kevin was calling to the other boy, "We've got to hurry and get out of here before someone sees us!" when he turned and saw Steve. For a moment he seemed stunned. Then he said, "I'll explain later, but come on and help us and we'll split the money with you."

"I can't do that!" Steve stammered.

"Then go on and get out of here," shouted Kevin. "But if you say anything to anyone, I'll tell them you helped us!"

The next morning the principal came around to all of the classrooms and announced that the school had been broken into. He talked about how there was more and more school vandalism and thefts taking place. And he said that if that kind of thing was ever going to be stopped, people were going to have to care enough to come forward with information that would help the police. He asked anyone who had information about the burglary to talk to him in confidence sometime during the day.

WHAT MIGHT STEVE DO?

24   GOMUKU

Materials needed
unlined paper *or* graph paper
pencil
Optional: ruler

☐   total group activity
☐   individual activity
☒   partner activity

Partner Activity

This activity provides practice in developing strategy. Gomuku is an old Japanese game similar to Tic-Tac-Toe. Students may use graph paper for a gameboard or may make their own gameboard by drawing from ten to twenty lines down and ten to twenty lines across.

One player writes *X*'s and the other writes *O*'s. The partners take turns writing their mark anywhere on the gameboard. The first player to get five marks in a row, horizontally, vertically, or diagonally, wins the game.

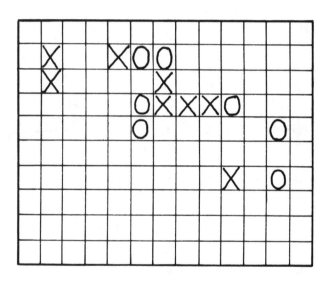

25   LINES AND DOTS

Materials needed
unlined paper
pencil
Optional: ruler

☐   total group activity
☐   individual activity
☒   partner activity

Partner Activity

This activity provides practice in developing strategy. Have one of the students draw a series of dots in evenly spaced rows. The number of rows is optional. Partners should then take turns drawing a horizontal or vertical line between two dots. When a student draws a line which completes a box, his or her first initial is written in the box and the player gets another turn. When all dots have been connected, the players count the number of boxes that have their initials. The player with the highest score wins.

Variation: An alternate way to play this game is to have students use colors to make their boxes. Each player selects one color for drawing lines. When a student completes a box in his or her color (with all four sides the same color), his or her first initial is written in the box and the player receives another turn. The player with the most initialed boxes wins.

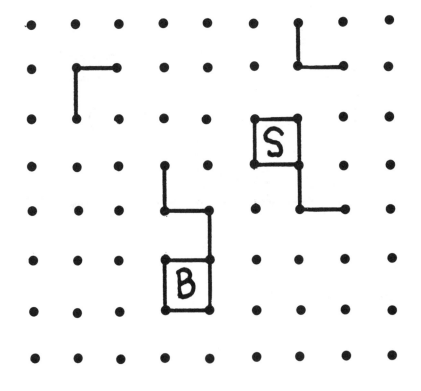

26   CIRCLES, CIRCLES, CIRCLES

Materials needed
unlined paper
pencil
Optional: compass

☐ total group activity
☒ individual activity
☐ partner activity

Individual Activity

This activity provides practice in creative thinking.

The student folds a piece of paper in half four times to make sixteen sections. He or she then draws a circle approximately one inch in diameter in each space. The challenge is to see how many different things the circles can be turned into. Stress that each circle should be an integral part of the drawing.

Variation: Instead of circles, have the students draw ovals and turn them into faces that have a variety of features and expressions.

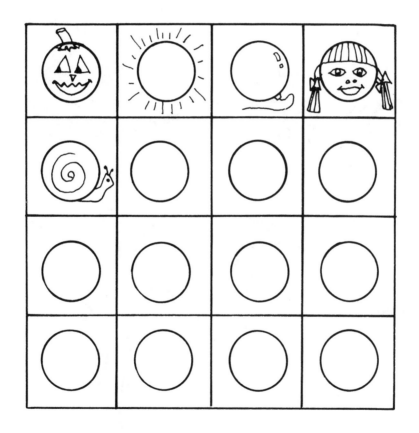

27 ALPHABET OBJECTS

Materials needed
unlined paper
pencil
Optional: crayons

☐ total group activity
☒ individual activity
☐ partner activity

Individual Activity

This activity provides practice in creative thinking.

The student writes five or six letters of the alphabet in manuscript or cursive with each letter well spaced across a piece of paper. He or she then uses each letter as the base for an illustration. **Note:** This activity can be worked on for a few minutes at a time for many days until the entire alphabet has been illustrated.

28 NIM

Materials needed
unlined paper
pencil
Optional: ruler

☐ total group activity
☒ individual activity
☒ partner activity

Partner Activity

This activity provides practice in developing strategy.

Nim is a very old game that is usually played with objects, but it can easily be played with paper and pencil. The object of the game is *not* to be the person to write an *X* in the last space. Students draw the following diagram and take turns writing either one, two, or three *X*'s in any *one* row on a single turn. They continue taking turns until only one empty space remains. The person who is forced to write an *X* in the last space loses the game.

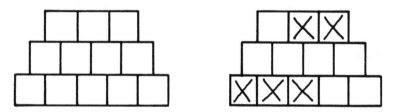

Variation: Although the most common form of Nim uses the above arrangement, made with rows of three, four, and five boxes, other combinations can be used. Students might like to try a combination of two, three, and four boxes, or five, six, and seven boxes (see below).

Encourage them to develop a strategy for winning the game. With perseverance, they'll discover several surefire ways of winning.

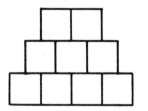 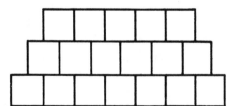

Adaptation for an Individual Student

Materials needed
unlined paper
2 different colored pencil, pens, *or* crayons
Optional: ruler

An individual student can practice strategies for winning the game by following the above procedures and using two different colors of pencils, pens, or crayons to represent the two players.

29   STRING OF DOTS

Materials needed
paper
pencil

☒   total group activity
☒   individual activity
☒   partner activity

Partner Activity

This activity provides practice in developing strategy.

Students draw a string of fifteen to thirty dots. They then take turns crossing off either one, two, or three dots on a single turn. (The dots need *not* be next to one another.) The person who crosses off the last dot loses.

Encourage students to develop a strategy for winning instead of crossing off dots randomly. Having the entire class play against the teacher is an excellent way to stimulate interest in strategies (see Total Group Adaptation).

• • • ✗ ✗ ✗ • • • ✗ ✗ • • • ✗

Total Group Adaptation

Materials needed
chalkboard
chalk
eraser

Write from fifteen to thirty dots on the chalkboard and play the above game, challenging students to try to beat you. When it is the class's turn, a student should come to the board and erase any one, two, or three dots. Or, if you prefer, have them stay seated and tell you which dots to erase.

The "magic number technique" of winning the game is to *leave nine dots*, then *five dots*, and finally *one dot*. For instance, if there are eleven dots remaining, erase two, leaving nine dots. If the students erase one dot, leaving eight dots, you should erase two dots, so that five dots remain. Once there are five dots left, there is no way the other person or team can win, as long as you remember to leave them just one dot. Try it and see!

✗ ✗ ✗ • • • ✗ ✗ ✗ ✗ • • ✗ ✗ ✗

Adaptation for an Individual Student

Materials needed
paper
2 different colored pencils, pens, *or* crayons

If you have not explained the "magic number technique" for winning, an individual student can experiment with various game strategies by using two different colored pencils, pens, or crayons to represent the two players.

30   THE WHEEL GAME

Materials needed
unlined paper
pencil
Optional: compass
Optional: ruler

☐ total group activity
☐ individual activity
☒ partner activity

Partner Activity

This activity provides practice in developing strategy.

One player draws a wheel, varying the number of spokes from game to game. The partners decide who writes *X*'s and who writes *O*'s. They then alternate turns, writing a total of three *X*'s or *O*'s during each turn. All three marks may be made within one section, or they may be spread out in two or three *adjacent* sections.

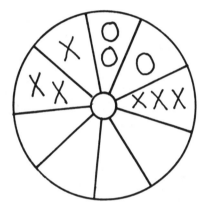

The person who puts his or her mark in the last spoke section wins. Encourage students to experiment with various strategies for winning the game.

Variation: A wheel is drawn, again with a different number of spokes in each game. One person writes *X*'s and the other *O*'s. On each turn, players may write one, two, or three of their marks; however, only *one* mark should be written in any section. The person who puts his or her mark in the last spoke section wins.

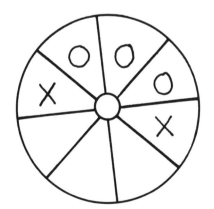

31   PASS THE ERASER

Materials needed
chalk eraser

X	total group activity
☐	individual activity
☐	partner activity

Total Group Activity

Have students count by twos, sixes, tens, or whatever multiple you choose. Hand a chalk eraser to one student and announce the first number and the count, for example, "200, count by ten." The student is to say the next number in the series and hand the eraser to the nearest student, who follows with the next number. Continue until the eraser has been passed to everyone in the class. Work for speed on this activity.

32   COMPUTER PUZZLE

Materials needed
chalkboard
chalk
eraser

☒ total group activity
☐ individual activity
☐ partner activity

Total Group Activity

On the chalkboard draw a box with dials and buttons on it, similar to the one shown here. Tell students that it is like a computer that will "do something" to numbers. To illustrate, draw a card with a 7 on it above the computer, and a card with a 10 on it below the computer. Ask, "What did the computer do to my number?" **(added 3)**. Help students realize that if the resulting number is larger, the computer is adding or multiplying. If the resulting number is smaller, the computer is subtracting or dividing.

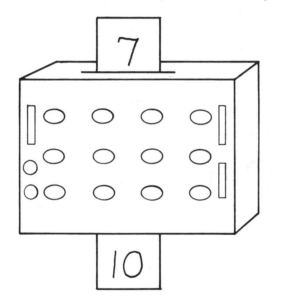

Erase the first set of numerals and write a 12 above the computer and an 8 below it. Ask, "What did the computer do this time?" **(subtracted 4)**. Continue this procedure until the children can quickly and easily determine the relationship between the top and bottom numerals. Use operations suitable for the age and ability levels of your students.

Variation: Draw the illustration of the computer described above on the chalkboard, telling the students that you are going to put different numbers into the computer and that the computer is programmed to do the *same thing* to each of the numbers. Example: Write a 2 on the card at the top of the computer and an 8 below it. Give the students a chance to study this transaction **(+ 6)**, but tell them to keep their discovery a secret. Remind them that the computer is going to treat the next calculation exactly the same way. Draw a 4 going into the computer and a 10 coming out. Again ask them to study the two numerals and keep the answer **(+ 6)** a secret.

Write a 5 on the top card and ask who could write or tell what number will come out **(11)**. Continue to use the add 6 pattern several more times. Then "reset" the computer to do something different, such as subtract 4, and move on to another group of numbers. Again, use operations that provide a challenge for your students.

33   INPUT—OUTPUT

Materials needed
chalkboard
chalk
eraser

☒ total group activity
☐ individual activity
☐ partner activity

Total Group Activity

Draw this simple "computer" illustration on the chalkboard, and ask students to study the number patterns. Call on a volunteer to fill in the next answer (**8**). Have the same student write a new numeral below the 4 and then choose another child to come to the chalkboard. Continue until the entire grid is filled in. The student who completes the grid should also fill in the button at the top right side of the illustration, indicating the "magic" number and process (**+4**).

Use a variety of patterns for the grid: adding, subtracting, multiplying, dividing, doubling the initial number, doubling the number and adding one more, and so on. Use operations and patterns that provide a challenge for the age and ability levels of your students.

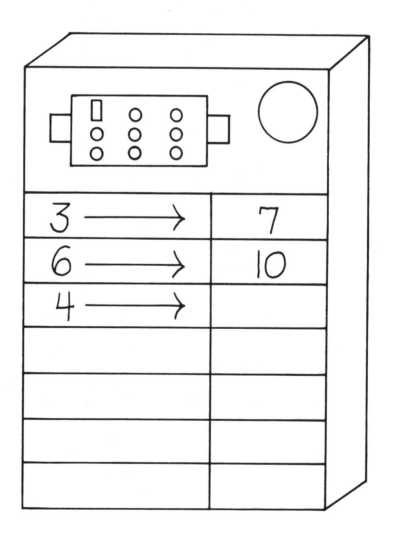

34   BUZZ

Materials needed
none

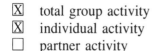

☒ total group activity
☒ individual activity
☐ partner activity

Total Group Activity

This is a fun activity that can be adapted to meet a variety of ability levels.

Students count from 1 to 100. Before they begin counting, the teacher designates a number. Whenever they come to a multiple of that number, they say "buzz" instead of the actual number. If 3 were the designated number, students would count as follows:

> 1, 2, buzz, 4, 5, buzz, 7, 8, buzz, and so on.

Variation: When students can easily count in the above manner, add the stipulation that they must also say "buzz" when the designated number is part of the answer. If 3 were the designated number, they would say "buzz" for the numbers 13, 23, 33, and so on, as well as for all numbers that are multiples of 3. The counting would go as follows:

> 1, 2, buzz, 4, 5, buzz, 7, 8, buzz, 10, 11, buzz, buzz, 14, buzz, 16, 17, buzz, 19, 20, buzz, 22, buzz, buzz, and so on.

Variation: Older Students can be given the additional challenge of distinguishing between the two types of responses described above. If 4 were the designated number, have them continue to say "buzz" for multiples of 4, and "Busy" if the answer has a 4 in it. If the number has a 4 in it, *and* is a multiple of 4, they should say "Busy-buzz." The counting for this version would go as follows:

> 1, 2, 3, busy-buzz, 5, 6, 7, buzz, 9, 10, 11, buzz, 13, busy, 15, buzz, 17, 18, 19, buzz, 21, 22, 23, busy-buzz, and so on.

Adaptation for an Individual Student

Materials needed
paper
pen *or* pencil
Optional: clock *or* timer

Assign a number or have the student select one. He or she follows the above procedure, writing the answers instead of saying them. The activity can be timed for an additional challenge.

35 DISCOVER MY PATTERN

Materials needed
chalkboard
chalk
eraser

[X] total group activity
[ ] individual activity
[ ] partner activity

Total Group Activity

Write the beginning of a number pattern on the board, for example:

18, 15, 12, _____, _____, _____,

Call on students to name each succeeding number. If the students are unsure of the pattern, remind them to look at the first two numerals and determine what happened between them. They should ask themselves questions like: Is the second number larger or smaller? How much larger or smaller? Which math operation was used to make it larger or smaller? Write the resulting answer between each pair of two numerals. Continue until the pattern emerges. For example:

$$-3 \qquad -3$$
18,   15,   12, _____, _____, _____,

Continue in the same manner using the following patterns. Use operations and patterns that provide a challenge for your students.

Discover the Pattern

$$+4 \qquad +4$$
(1) 12,   16,   20, _____, _____, _____,

$$\times 2 \quad \times 2 \quad \times 2$$
(2) 3,   6,   12,   24, _____, _____, _____,

$$+2 \quad -1 \quad +2 \quad -1$$
(3) 1,   3,   2,   4,   3, _____, _____, _____,

$$+4 \quad -2 \quad +4 \quad -2$$
(4) 12,   16,   14,   18,   16, _____, _____, _____,

$$\times 4 \quad \div 2 \quad \times 4 \quad \div 2$$
(5) 4,   16,   8,   32,   16, _____, _____, _____,

36   PLACE VALUE NUMBER SEARCH

Materials needed
chalkboard
chalk
eraser
4 or 5 sheets of paper
pencil

☒ total group activity
☐ individual activity
☐ partner activity

Total Group Activity

Enlist a volunteer to come to the chalkboard and draw three vertical lines. Meanwhile, on a piece of paper secretly write a three-digit numeral large enough to be seen at the back of the room. Stand with your back to the student at the chalkboard, holding the numeral so that it can be seen by the class. Describe your number as in this example: "My number has 3 in the hundred's place. Write that in the proper location. My number has 7 in the one's place. Write that in the correct place. My number has 4 in the ten's place. Where does that belong?" After the student has written the last digit, ask the child to read the numeral on the chalkboard (**347**). If the numeral is correct, reveal your numeral and enjoy the delight on the student's face when he or she discovers the numerals match. If the numerals do not match, reread the description again for a second try. The student at the chalkboard can then select the next child to go to the board.

Once the children understand the process, let them take turns giving the clues to the student at the chalkboard.

Sample Clues:
My number is in the ten's place and is worth 70. (**70**)
My number is in the hundred's place and its value is 800. (**800**)

37   NUMBER-IN-A-BOX

Materials needed
box *or* paper bag
paper
pencil
Optional: Number-Blox™ *or* other commercial place-value blocks

☒   total group activity
☐   individual activity
☒   partner activity

Total Group Activity

On a slip of paper write a numeral and one way to make its value using only ones and tens. For example:

43 = 3 tens and 13 ones

Place the slip of paper in a box or bag. If you have Number-Blox™ or other place-value blocks, place these equivalents in the box or bag instead of writing the value on paper.

Tell the students, "I have a number in the box. I've used only ones and tens to make the number. It is worth 43 ones. What do I have in the box?" If the children guess 4 tens and 3 ones, answer, "That is one way to make 43, but that's not what is in the box. What is another way I might make 43 using ones and tens?" When the number has been guessed correctly, show them the answer.

Choose a student to lead the next game.

Partner Adaptation

Materials needed
paper
pencils

The first player says a number between 10 and 99, then secretly writes the numeral and one way to make its value. For example:

73 = 5 tens and 23 ones

The other player tries to guess how the number was made. Each time the student guesses, the first player makes a tally mark. Play continues until the student guesses correctly. The roles are then reversed. The first person to have twenty-five tally marks loses the game.

To make this a silent activity, have the students *write* their guesses and the corresponding responses.

38 DIGIT DETECTIVE

Materials needed:
chalkboard *or* paper
chalk *or* pencils

☒ total group activity
☐ individual activity
☒ partner activity

Total Group Activity

Secretly write a two-digit number on a piece of paper or on the chalkboard in a place that can be hidden. (Do not write a number that repeats the same digits, for example, 55. Challenge students to guess your number by writing the following clues on the chalkboard after each guess. Use the following code:

☆ correct digit in the correct place
↶ correct digit in the wrong place
X nothing right

Example: (The secret number is 54.)

Guess 1 ——— 25 ↶ (Indicates it could be either a 5 in the ten's place or a 2 in the one's place.)

Guess 2 ——— 62 X (Now you know it must be 5 in the ten's place.)

Guess 3 ——— 47 ↶ (Since you know 5 will be in the ten's place, the 7 can't move to that position. Therefore the 4 must be the digit that needs to move...Aha!)

Guess 4 ——— 54 ☆ ☆ (Eureka!)

Variation: When students become proficient with two-digit numbers, try the same activity with three-digit numbers. Use the same code with the following additions.

☆ ☆ two correct digits in the correct place

☆ ↶ two correct digits, one in the right place, one in the wrong place

↶ ↶ two correct digits, both in the wrong place

☆ ☆ ↶ three correct digits, two in the right place, one in the wrong place

☆ ↶ ↶ three correct digits, one in the right place, two in the wrong place

↶ ↶ ↶ three correct digits, all three in the wrong place

Partner Adaptation

Materials needed
paper
pencils

Partners follow the above directions, taking turns providing the secret number. To make this a silent activity, have the students write their guesses and the corresponding responses.

39   WHICH IS WHICH?

Materials needed
½ sheet of lined paper for each student
pencil for each student

☒ total group activity
☐ individual activity
☐ partner activity

Total Group Activity

Dictate eight to ten numbers which students write vertically on a half sheet of paper, leaving a line between each as shown here. Remind students that even numbers end with 0, 2, 4, 6, or 8. Ask the students to write the heading "Even." Then have them circle each even numeral and underline the digit that determined it was an even number.

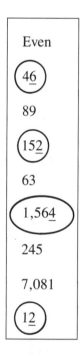

When they have completed this task, have them turn the paper over and write the heading "Odd." Remind them that odd numbers end with 1, 3, 5, 7, or 9. Dictate a new set of numbers and have them circle each numeral that made that determination.

Check all answers on the chalkboard, inviting student participation.

40   QUICKIE GRAPHS

Materials needed
chalkboard
chalk
eraser
Optional: ruler *or* yardstick

☒ total group activity
☐ individual activity
☐ partner activity

Total Group Activity

Draw a horizontal or vertical bar graph on the chalkboard and ask questions related to one of the following topics, such as "How many of you have brown hair?" **(15)** "How many have blond hair?" and so on, for the graph "Color of hair."

Count the number of raised hands and plot the information on the graph. When the graph is completed, encourage the students to interpret the information by asking questions such as, "How many people have brown hair?" **(15)**, Do more people have black hair or red hair?" **(black)**, and so on.

Variation: Leave the graph on the chalkboard. Have the students copy the graph and record the answers to the interpretive questions you ask.

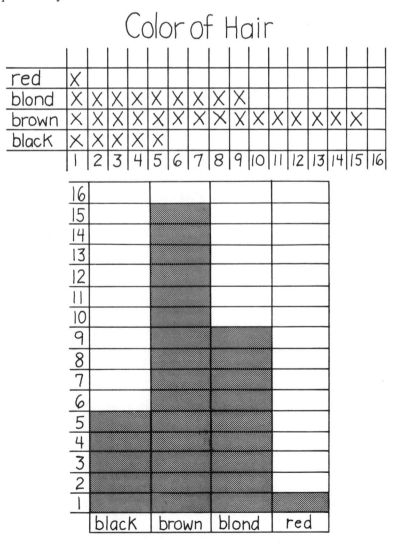

Quickie Graph Topics

1. number of baby teeth lost
2. number of brothers or sisters
3. number of pets
4. number of letters in first name *or* in last name
5. number of buttons
6. color of eyes
7. color of hair
8. month of birthday
9. how they come to school (bus, walk, bike, car)
10. shoe size
11. what grade they were in when they started attending present school
12. lunches (bought, brought in a bag, brought in a lunch box, went home)
13. favorite cold cereal
14. favorite recess activity
15. favorite T.V. show on a specific day
16. favorite sports
17. favorite T.V. *or* sports star

41   COORDINATE TIC-TAC-TOE

Materials needed
chalkboard
chalk
eraser
Optional: ruler *or* yardstick

☒ total group activity
☐ individual activity
☒ partner activity

Total Group Activity

Divide the class into two teams of *X*'s and *O*'s. Draw a grid four lines across and four lines down, numbering the lines vertically and horizontally 0 to 3, as shown in the illustration. Remind students that when coordinates are given, the number for the horizontal axis always comes first, then the number for the vertical axis. Teams alternate calling out coordinates, for example "1, 2," indicating where you should write their team's symbol of *X* or *O*. The first team with three of their marks in a row wins.

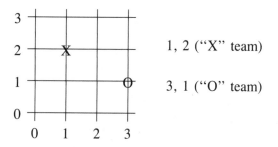

1, 2 ("X" team)

3, 1 ("O" team)

After several games, expand the grid to six lines across and six lines down and play a game of four in a row.

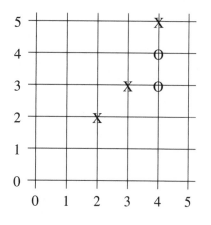

Partner Adaptation

Materials needed
unlined paper
pencils
Optional: ruler

One of the partners draws a grid either four lines across and four lines down, numbered 0 to 3, or six lines across and six lines down, numbered 0 to 5. One player writes X's and the other writes O's.

On each turn, before an X or O is written, the student must say the coordinates. If coordinates are inadvertently called whose intersection is at a different location than what was intended, the student must still write the X or O at the position that was stated. This will encourage the caller to make his move carefully.

Students alternate turns until one of them has three marks in a row if using the four-line grid, or four marks in a row if using the six-line grid. The loser goes first in the next game.

To make this a silent activity, have players *write* the coordinates on each turn instead of saying them aloud.

42   FIND THE SQUARE

Materials needed
chalkboard
chalk
eraser
unlined paper
pencil
Optional: ruler *or* yardstick

☒ total group activity
☐ individual activity
☒ partner activity

Total Group Activity

Draw a ten-square by ten-square grid on the chalkboard and number each of the lines from 0 to 10 as shown here. Make a duplicate grid on a piece of paper and draw a square somewhere on this grid. Make the sides of the square correspond with the lines on the grid. (See the teacher's grid below.)

Chalkboard Grid   **Teacher's Grid**

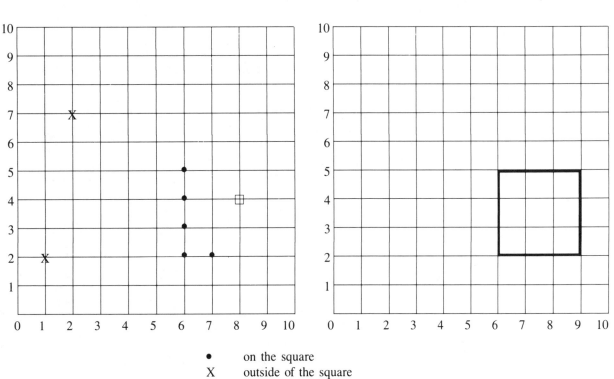

•   on the square
X   outside of the square
☐   inside of the square

Challenge students to find the location of your square by naming coordinates for their guesses. (Remind them to give coordinates by saying the horizontal axis first, then the vertical axis.) As they say coordinates, use the code shown below the sample grids to indicate whether the guess is *on* the square, *outside* of the square, or *inside* of the square. Write the appropriate code mark on the chalkboard grid.

After a few rounds, some of the students will realize that once the location and length of *one* side of the square is located, all that needs to be found is the *direction* of the remainder of the square. The other sides can then be determined easily, since they will be the same length.

Follow-Up Activity: At a later date hide a rectangle, rather than a square, and have students use the knowledge gained from "Find the Square" to develop strategies for finding the rectangle.

Partner Variation

Materials needed
unlined paper
pencils
Optional: ruler

Students follow the above directions but play the game with a partner.

43   LOOK, THINK, ANSWER

Materials needed
chalkboard
chalk
eraser

☒ total group activity
☐ individual activity
☐ partner activity

Total Group Activity

On the chalkboard draw the beginning of a chart similar to the ones shown below and describe the situation it illustrates. For example:

A school is having a carnival. Tickets for one game or activity booth cost 15¢.

tickets	1	2	3	4	5	6	7	8	9	10
cost	15¢	30¢								

Have the students complete the chart, then answer interpretive questions such as:

—A child wants to buy 5 tickets. How much will that cost? **(75¢)**

—If I had 45¢, how many tickets could I buy? **(3)**

—Terry bought 3 tickets for himself and 3 tickets for his little brother. How much money did he spend? **(90¢)**

Topics for Charts

1. Steve's family is going to take a trip. In past years they've found they usually travel 50 miles in one hour. If they continue to travel at the same speed, how many miles will they travel in 5 hours? **(250)** How many hours will it take for them to travel 350 miles? **(7)** . . .

hours	1	2	3	4	5	6	7	8	9	10
miles	50	100								

2. Jane is going to have a birthday party. She knows that one bottle of juice will fill 6 glasses. If she wants to fill 24 glasses, how many bottles should she buy? **(4)** If she bought 7 bottles, how many glasses could she fill? **(42)**...

bottles	1	2	3	4	5	6	7	8
glasses	6	12						

3. Eric found that it takes him 3 minutes to walk 1 block. How far can he walk in 15 minutes? **(5)** If he walks for 24 minutes, how many blocks will he have traveled? **(8)**...

blocks	1	2	3	4	5	6	7	8	9	10
minutes	3	6								

4. John wants to buy some favors for a party. There are 2 favors in each package. If John wants 12 favors, how many packages will he need to buy? **(6)** If he buys 8 packages, how many favors will he have? **(16)**...

packages	1	2	3	4	5	6	7	8
favors	2	4						

44   TABLE TEASERS

Materials needed
chalkboard
chalk
eraser

☒ total group activity
☐ individual activity
☐ partner activity

Total Group Activity

On the chalkboard draw a table similar to the ones shown below and tell the brief story about its meaning. For example:

Jake decided to keep a record of how many points his team scored during each basketball game.

Game	1	2	3	4	5	6
Points	32	45	26	44	38	36

Ask interpretive questions such as:

—In which game did Jake's team get the most points? **(game 2)**

—In which game did they get the least points? **(game 3)**

—Did they score more points in game 1 or in game 3? **(game 1)**

Topics for Tables

The following tables are presented in two forms: basic and extended formats. Choose whichever is most appropriate for your students.

1. A group of children decided to keep a record of how many pages they read in their library books each week. Did Sam or Jane read more pages? **(Sam)** John read fewer pages than Jane. How many fewer? **(3)** . . .

Pages Read

Sam	John	Kim	Dan	Jane	Kristin
59	42	37	63	45	25

Extended format:

Did Dan read more pages the first week or the second week? (**first week**) How many pages did Jane read all together? (**105**) Who read more the second week, Sam or Kristin? (**Sam**)...

Pages Read

	Sam	John	Kim	Dan	Jane	Kristin
Week 1	59	42	37	63	45	25
Week 2	45	57	30	58	60	34

2. Six children wanted to find out how many hours they watched T.V. each week. Who watched the most T.V.? (**Jean**) Who watched the least amount of T.V.? (**Dan**) Did Kathy or Kirk spend more time watching T.V.? (**Kathy**)...

Hours Spent Watching T.V.

Kirk	Jane	Dan	Kathy	Mary	Jean
35	23	7	54	14	67

Extended format:

Who watched the least amount of T.V. during the first week? (**Dan**) Did Kirk watch more T.V. the first week or the second week? (**second week**) Who watched the most T.V. the second week? (**Jean**) How many children watched less T.V. the second week? (**3—Kirk, Kathy, Jean**)...

Hours Spent Watching T.V.

	Kirk	Jane	Dan	Kathy	Mary	Jean
Week 1	25	23	7	54	14	67
Week 2	19	26	7	50	15	59

3. Mr. Columbo told his class they could earn bonus points during the following two months. At the end of the first month some of the children compared the points they had earned. Who earned the most points? (**Sarah**) Who earned the fewest points? (**Julie**) Did Brian or Brandon earn more points? (**Brandon**)...

Bonus Points

Julie	Brandon	Chris	Tom	Brian	Sarah
42	83	67	59	75	84

Extended format:

Who had the most bonus points for the two-month period? **(Sarah)** Who had the fewest points for the two months? **(Julie)** Did Brian or Brandon have more points the second month? **(Brian)** . . .

Bonus Points

	Julie	Brandon	Chris	Tom	Brian	Sarah
First month	42	83	67	59	75	84
Second month	65	78	65	70	84	79

4. Greenfield School was having a fair. Six children sold tickets. At the end of the day they compared their sales. Did Jason or Shane sell more tickets? **(Jason)** Who sold the fewest tickets? **(John)** Jason sold more tickets than Terra. How many more? **(4)** . . .

Tickets Sold

Shane	Terra	John	Jason	Lori	Angie
201	198	123	202	154	179

Extended format:

Who sold the fewest tickets in all? **(John)** Who sold the most? **(Jason)** During the afternoon, did Shane or Lori sell more tickets? **(Shane)** John and Jason worked in the same booth. How many tickets did they sell in their booth during the morning? **(145)** . . .

Tickets Sold

	Shane	Terra	John	Jason	Lori	Angie
Morning	98	93	82	63	90	103
Afternoon	103	105	41	139	64	76

45   CALENDAR SEARCH

Materials needed
chalkboard
chalk
calendar
   or
calendar posted in room

☒ total group activity
☐ individual activity
☐ partner activity

Total Group Activity

Draw a calendar of the current month on the chalkboard or post a calendar where all students can see it. Randomly call on students to answer the following questions. (This activity can be repeated each month.)

Calendar Search Questions

1. How many _____ (Saturdays, Mondays, etc.) are there this month?
2. What is the first *day* of the month?
3. What is the last *day* of the month?
4. Fred has a soccer (baseball, football, basketball) game every Thursday. How many games will he play this month?
5. What *date* is the second Tuesday of this month?
6. What *day* is the 10th of this month?
7. What day is today? Sam is going to a birthday party (skating, skiing, to visit his grandmother, to the movies, etc.) on _____ 19th. How many days does he have to wait?
                        (month)

   On what *day* will the party be?
8. How many *full* weeks are there this month?
9. How many days have passed since _____?
10. What is the date a week before the 15th? What is the date a week after the 15th?
11. (Discuss holidays and special days that fall during the current month. For example: Halloween is on October 31. What *day* will that be? and so on.

46 MONTHS, SEASONS, AND SPECIAL DAYS

Materials needed

chalkboard
chalk
eraser
  or
poster paper *or* paper
crayon, pen, *or* pencil

☒ total group activity
☐ individual activity
☐ partner activity

Total Group Activity

Ask students to describe each month of the year, including the names of special days that fall during the month, the season of the year, the number of days, and so on. Ask questions to draw out the information they omit. A summary of each month follows as a reference. Have a student record the descriptions as they are formulated. If you are working with younger students, you may want to write the information on the chalkboard or on sheets of poster paper so it can be used as a reference.

Begin the game by choosing a student to name a month. Call on another student, then slowly count to 10. By the count of 10, the second player must say a fact about the designated month. ("Halloween is in October," "October has 31 days," and so on.)

If the second player succeeds, he or she begins the next turn by naming the same month or a different month and repeating the above procedure. If an incorrect answer or repeated answer is given, or there is no response by the count of 10, the calling player continues his or her turn.

The same fact may not be given twice in the game. However, if a month is named and the player feels that all of the information about that month has already been given, the student may say, "I challenge." The player who named the month must give a fact about the month or lost his turn to the challenger, who gets to continue the game.

Because the descriptions of each month may take some time to elicit, the gathering of monthly descriptions could take place during one segment of time and the playing of the game during another. It will also be useful to have one student act as "fact-keeper" to check off facts given on the list provided here or on a student-recorded list so that no fact is repeated.

January

31 days
Winter
Jan. 1–New Year's Day
Jan. 15–Dr. Martin Luther King's birthday
Chinese New Year (movable date, Jan. or Feb.)

February

28 days, except 29 days during leap year
Winter
Feb. 2–Groundhog Day
Feb. 12–Abraham Lincoln's birthday
Feb. 14–Valentine's Day
Feb. 22–George Washington's birthday
Chinese New Year (movable date, Jan. or Feb.)

March

31 days
beginning of Spring
Mar. 7–Arbor Day (movable date, according to state)
Mar. 17–St. Patrick's Day
Passover (movable date, Mar. or Apr.)
Easter (movable date, Mar. or Apr.)

April

30 days
Spring
Apr. 1–April Fools' Day
Passover (movable date, Mar. or Apr.)
Easter (movable date, Mar. or Apr.)

May

31 days
Spring
Mother's Day (second Sunday)
Victoria Day (Canada—Monday preceding May 25)
Memorial Day (last Monday)

June

30 days
beginning of Summer
June 14–Flag Day
Father's Day (third Sunday)

July

31 days
Summer
July 1–Dominion Day (Canada)
July 4–Independence Day

August

31 days
Summer

September

30 days
beginning of Fall
Labor Day (first Monday)
Rosh Hashanah (movable date)
Yom Kippur (movable date, Sept. or Oct.)

October

31 days
Fall
Columbus Day (second Monday)
Thanksgiving (Canada-second Monday)
Oct. 31–Halloween
Yom Kippur (movable date, Sept. or Oct.)
Baseball's World Series (movable dates)

November

30 days
Fall
Nov. 11–Veterans' Day
Election Day (second Tuesday)
Thanksgiving (fourth Thursday)

December

31 days
beginning of Winter
Dec. 25–Christmas
Hanukkah (movable date)

47   LISTEN AND SOLVE

Materials needed
chalkboard
chalk
eraser
  or
clock with movable hands

[X] total group activity
[ ] individual activity
[ ] partner activity

Total Group Activity

Clocks may be drawn on the chalkboard to demonstrate answers to the following questions, or a clock with movable hands may be used. Younger students would benefit from actually manipulating a movable clock or coming to the board to draw the clock's hands.

Two different times are given for each problem. The first time involves only hours, half hours, or quarter hours. The second time, in parentheses, requires a greater understanding of time. Choose the exercise most appropriate for your students' abilities.

Follow-Up Activity: At a later date ask the same series of questions using different names, circumstances, and times. As students become confident with questions of this type, repeat the activity and have them record their answers on half sheets of lined paper.

Set the Clock and Tell the Time

1. Draw a clock on the chalkboard that shows *3 o'clock*.
   A. Carl went to his friend's house at this time. He played for *two hours* (1 hr. 20 min.). What time did he leave his friend's house? (**5:00** *or* **4:20**)
   B. Carl will get out of school in half an hour. (40 min.). What time will he get out of school? (**3:30** *or* **3:40**)
   C. He'll eat dinner in *3 hours* (3 hr. 20 min.). What time will he eat? (**6:00** *or* **6:20**)
   D. He'll go to bed in *5 hours* (5 hr. 45 min.). What time will he go to bed? (**8:00** *or* **8:45**)

2. Draw a clock on the chalkboard that shows *7 o'clock*.
   A. This is the time when Sally got up this morning. It took her *30 minutes* (45 min.) to wash and get dressed. At what time was she dressed? (**7:30** *or* **7:45**)
   B. It took her another *30 minutes* (20 min.) to eat breakfast. At what time was she finished eating? (**8:00** *or* **8:05**)
   C. She left for school *1 hour* (1 hr. 20 min.) after she got up. What time did she leave for school? (**8:00** *or* **8:20**)
   D. It took her *30 minutes* (20 min.) to walk to school. What time did she get there? (**8:30** *or* **8:40**)

3. Draw a clock on the chalkboard that shows *10 o'clock*.
   A. Sam and his parents are going to take a trip (skiing, camping, visiting his grandparents). They want to leave at this time (10:00 o'clock). They think it will take them *1 hour* (1 hr. 25 min.) to get dressed, have breakfast, and pack up the car. What time will they need to get up? (**9:00** *or* **8:35**)
   B. They got away right on time. After *1½ hours* (2 hr. 40 min.) they stopped at a gas station. What time was it? (**11:30** *or* **12:40**)

C. They stayed at the gas station for *15 minutes* (10 min.). What time did they leave the station? **(11:45 *or* 12:50)**

D. They finally arrived at their destination *1 hour* (1 hr. 10 min.) later. What time did they get there? **(12:45 *or* 2:00)**

4. Draw a clock on the chalkboard that shows *1 o'clock*.

    A. This is the time right now. Jane has a softball game (soccer game, flag football game) in *1 hour 15 minutes* (1 hr. 45 min.). What time will the game be? **(2:15 *or* 2:45)**

    B. The game is supposed to last about *2 hours* (2 hr. 20 min.). What time should it be over? **(4:15 *or* 5:05)**

5. Draw a clock on the chalkboard that shows *3:30*.

    A. Nancy has a piano lesson (skating lesson, guitar lesson) at this time. She has to wait for *2 hours* (2 hr. 5 min.) until it will be time for her lesson. What time is it now? **(1:30 *or* 1:25)**

    B. If her lesson lasts *half an hour* (45 min.) what time will it be over? **(4:00 *or* 4:15)**

6. Have students look at the classroom clock and identify the current time. Then ask a series a questions.

    A. If I am going to go home _____ (min./hr.) from now, what time will I leave?

    B. If we had had recess _____ (min./hr.) ago, what time would the recess have been?

    C. If John had come to school at 9:00 o'clock, how long would he have been at school?

    D. If we were going to have music (gym, art, go to the library, etc.) in _____ (min./hr.), what time would it be?

48   MYSTERY COINS

Materials needed
paper
pencil
Optional: small paper bag *or* box
Optional: variety of coins

☒ total group activity
☐ individual activity
☒ partner activity

Total Group Activity

On a piece of paper secretly write an amount of money and one way to make the total. For example:

$$35¢ = 3 \text{ dimes, 5 pennies}$$

Challenge the students to discover what is on the paper by saying, "I have *8 coins* with a total value of 35¢. What are my coins?" **(3 dimes, 5 pennies)**

Variation: Instead of writing the amount on a piece of paper, put the actual coins in a paper bag or box. Announce the total value and the number of coins. When the students determine the denominations of the hidden coins, validate their answer by showing them the actual money.

Partner Adaptation

Each player takes a piece of paper and writes an amount of money and one way to make the total. For example:

$$52¢ = 1 \text{ quarter, 2 dimes, 1 nickel, 2 pennies}$$

On the other side of the paper each writes the total value and the number of coins **(52¢, 6 coins).**

Players then exchange papers and race to see who can be the first to determine the answer to the opponent's puzzle. The winner receives one point. The first player with five points wins the game.

49   MAKING CHANGE

Materials needed
chalkboard
chalk
eraser
Optional: clock *or* timer

☒ total group activity
☐ individual activity
☐ partner activity

Total Group Activity

Tell the students, "I bought something that cost 60¢. I gave the salesperson _____ (either the amount, for example, 75¢, or the coins, H, Q—1 half dollar and 1 quarter). How much change did I receive?" **(15¢)** As you say each number, write it on the board. Continue with examples of this type until students become familiar with the process. Then divide the class into two teams and number the players.

Alternate giving problems to the teams as follows: Write the cost of the item in numerals and the amount given to the salesperson *either* in numerals or in code (N = nickel, D = dime, Q = quarter, H = half dollar, $ = dollar).

Team A's Player 1 gives the amount of change received for his problem. If correct, his team gets one point and play continues with Team B's Player 1. If incorrect, Player 1 on Team B gets a chance and, if correct, Team B gets the point. Then play continues with Player 2 on Team B. If Player 1 on Team B is unable to give the correct answer to Team A's question, no points are earned and Team B's Player 2 continues play.

The game ends when all students have had a turn or at the end of a designated time period. The team with the most points wins.

Sample problems are given in the chart on p. 79.

Variation (Grades 2–3)

Materials needed
chalkboard
chalk
eraser
½ sheet of lined paper for each student
pencil for each student

When working with younger students, instead of playing the game you may prefer to have students use a half sheet of lined paper and record their answers as you say each problem.

How Much Change Do I Receive?

	Cost	Gave Salesperson		Change
1.	22¢	D, D, N	(25¢)	3¢
2.	34¢	D, D, D, N	(35¢)	1¢
3.	41¢	Q, Q	(50¢)	9¢
4.	43¢	Q, D, D	(45¢)	2¢
5.	47¢	Q, D, D, N	(50¢)	3¢
6.	49¢	Q, Q	(50¢)	1¢
7.	56¢	H, D	(60¢)	4¢
8	65¢	H, Q	(75¢)	10¢
9.	79¢	H, Q, N	(80¢)	1¢
10.	84¢	H, Q, D, N	(90¢)	6¢
11.	93¢	H, Q, D, D	(95¢)	2¢
12.	94¢	H, Q, Q	($1.00)	6¢
13.	$1.05	H, H, Q	($1.25)	20¢
14.	$1.19	$1, Q	($1.25)	6¢
15.	$1.29	$1, Q, Q	($1.50)	21¢
16.	$1.35	$1, Q, Q	($1.50)	15¢
17.	$1.43	$1, Q, D, D, N	($1.50)	7¢
18	$1.59	$1, H, Q	($1.75)	16¢
19.	$1.79	$1, H, Q, N	($1.80)	1¢
20.	$1.85	$1, H, Q, D, N	($1.90)	5¢
21.	$1.93	$1, H, Q, Q	($2.00)	7¢
22.	$1.95	$1, H, H	($2.00)	5¢
23.	$1.98	$1, H, Q, Q	($2.00)	2¢
24.	$2.25	$2, Q, Q	($2.50)	25¢
25.	$2.35	$1, H, H, H	($2.50)	15¢
26.	$2.50	$2, H, Q, Q	($3.00)	50¢
27.	$2.59	$2, H, Q	($2.75)	16¢
28.	$2.79	$2, H, Q, Q	($3.00)	21¢
29.	$2.89	$2, H, H	($3.00)	11¢
30.	$3.49	$3, Q, D, D, N	($3.50)	1¢
31.	$3.79	$3, H, Q, D	($3.85)	6¢
32.	$4.59	$4, H, Q	($4.75)	16¢
33.	$4.65	$4, H, D, D, N	($4.75)	10¢
34.	$4.79	$4, H, Q, Q	($5.00)	21¢

50   INSIDE/OUTSIDE

Materials needed
chalkboard
chalk
eraser
½ sheet of paper for each student
pencil for each student

[X]   total group activity
[ ]   individual activity
[ ]   partner activity

Total Group Activity

Draw overlapping shapes on the chalkboard like the ones shown here. Put dots or a combination of dots, x's, and/or circles inside the shapes. Then ask interpretive questions such as these in the following example:

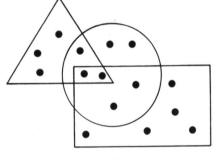

1. How many dots are in the circle? **(7)**
2. How many dots are in both the circle and the rectangle? **(4)**
3. How many dots are in the circle, rectangle, and triangle? **(2)**
4. How many dots are outside the circle? **(8)**
5. How many dots are in the rectangle, but not in the circle or triangle? **(5)**

If students are uncertain of how the answers were derived, have one student come to the chalkboard and trace the designated shape(s) with a finger and then identify the number of dots within the specified areas.

Once students understand the process, ask them to number a half sheet of paper from one to ten. Draw a new set of overlapping shapes on the chalkboard and ask similar questions, having the students record their answers on paper. Another sample is shown here.

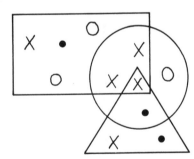

51 THREE-DIMENSIONAL SHAPE HUNT

Materials needed
chalkboard
chalk
eraser

X total group activity
X individual activity
☐ partner activity

Total Group Activity

On the chalkboard write the term for and draw each three-dimensional shape as illustrated below. Have the students look around the room and name objects that are the same shape. Then have them think of other things they have seen that are the same shape.

Follow-Up Activity: At a later date, review the above activity by challenging students to name *ten* things in each shape category. Write a three-dimensional shape on the chalkboard and make a tally mark each time a correct item is named.

Adaptation for an Individual Student

Materials needed
chalkboard
chalk
eraser
paper
pencil

Write the names of several three-dimensional shapes on the chalkboard and have the student list as many objects as he or she can think of for each of the designated shapes.

SHAPES:

Sphere

globe, doorknob, basketball, tennis ball, marble, grape

Rectangular prism

box, book, clock, door, chalk eraser

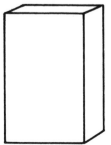

Triangular prism

block, roof of a house, piece of cake, tent, piece of pie

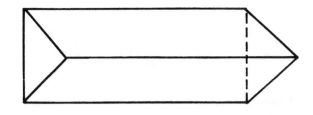

Cylinder

pointer, straw, tin can

Cube (six equal faces)

alphabet block, box, die, sugar cube, bouillon cube

Cone

tip of a pencil, nose cone on a rocket, party hat, tepee, top of a castle

Pyramid (each face is a triangle and the base is a polygon—a triangle, square, pentagon, etc.)

block, Egyptian pyramids, top of the Washington Monument

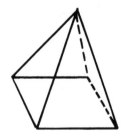
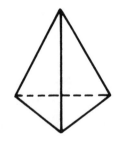

52   NAME MY SHAPE

Materials needed
chalkboard
chalk
eraser
½ sheet of paper for each student
pencil for each student
crayon for each student

|X| total group activity
|☐| individual activity
|☐| partner activity

Total Group Activity

On the chalkboard draw the illustrated shapes shown below and discuss each one. Then describe a "mystery" shape and have students try to identify it. Erase the board and draw one of the shapes. Have the students write its name, spelling it as best they can. Continue in this way until all shapes have been drawn. Students should correct their papers with crayons as you read the answers.

SHAPES:

1. Circle
   —a curved line forming a figure in which every point of the line is an equal distance from the center of the figure.

2. Triangle
   —a three-sided figure with three angles.

3. Square
   —a four-sided figure with all sides equal and two right angles.

4. Rectangle
   —a four-sided figure with opposite sides equal and two right angles.

5. Pentagon
   —a five-sided figure with five angles. (An easy way to draw a pentagon is to first draw a five-pointed star, then connect the outside points and erase the star.)

6. Hexagon
   —a six-sided figure with six angles.

7. Octagon
   —an eight-sided figure with eight angles.

8. Parallelogram
   —a four-sided figure with two sets of parallel sides. (Yes! A rectangle and a square are special types of parallelograms.)

9. Trapezoid
   —a four-sided figure with two parallel sides and two sides that are not parallel.

10. Rhomboid
    —a four-sided figure with two parallel sides of equal length and two other sides of equal length, but whose length differs from the first pair. (Another type of parallelogram.)

11. Rhombus
    —a four-sided figure with two pairs of equal sides, all of equal length, whose sides do not form right angles. (Students can easily tell whether or not a shape has a right angle by making an "L" shape with thumb and forefinger and comparing this to the angle in question.)

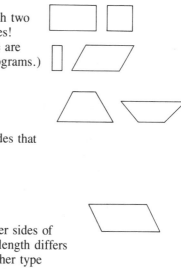

53 PERIMETER/AREA PUZZLERS

Materials needed
centimeter graph paper for each student
pencil for each student

☒ total group activity
☐ individual activity
☐ partner activity

Total Group Activity

Review the concept of square area (the measure of the bounded surface of a figure) with the students. Then designate a specific number of square units and have the students see how many different ways they can show this on centimeter graph paper. For example, 9 square centimeters may be expressed through several different shapes. Three are shown below.

9 SQ. CM   9 SQ. CM   9 SQ. CM

PERIMETER: 14   PERIMETER: 12   PERIMETER: 16

Review the concept of perimeter (the total length of the outer boundary of a figure) with the students. With centimeter graph paper it is easy to count the total number of centimeters that comprise the perimeter of a figure. The students should then write the perimeter beneath each figure they have drawn.

Variation (Grades 4–6)

Materials needed
centimeter graph paper for each student
pencil for each student

Students draw squares, rectangles, and triangles on centimeter graph paper, then use mathematical formulas to determine the area of each figure. Some examples are shown here.

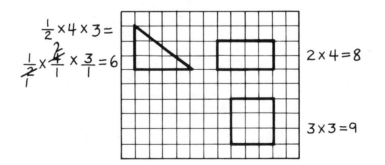

$$\frac{1}{2} \times 4 \times 3 =$$

$$\frac{1}{2} \times \frac{4}{1} \times \frac{3}{1} = 6$$

$$2 \times 4 = 8$$

$$3 \times 3 = 9$$

54 YOU WRITE THE GREATER THAN OR LESS THAN SIGN

Materials needed
chalkboard
chalk
eraser
Optional: ½ sheet of lined paper for each student
Optional: pencil for each student

☒ total group activity
☐ individual activity
☐ partner activity

Total Group Activity

Discuss the two symbols for "greater than" (>) and "less than" (<). Then write two numerals on the chalkboard. For example:

47   53

Have a volunteer write the appropriate greater than or less than symbol between the numerals (<). Ask, "How do you know that 47 is less than 53?" (**A number with 4 tens is less than a number with 5 tens.**) Use a diagram to demonstrate:

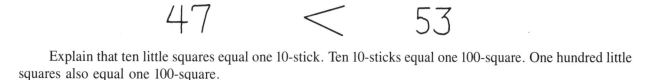

Explain that ten little squares equal one 10-stick. Ten 10-sticks equal one 100-square. One hundred little squares also equal one 100-square.

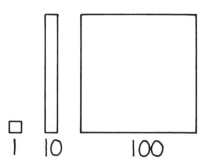

This activity provides a good opportunity to discuss numerals that often confuse children (for example, 1001 as opposed to 1010).

If time permits, write a pair of numerals on the chalkboard. On a half sheet of lined paper, have students copy the numeral and insert the appropriate greater than or less than symbol. Discuss the answer, then write two more numerals, continuing in the same manner.

55 GUESS MY NUMBER

Materials needed
chalkboard
chalk
eraser
Optional: a pencil and sheet of paper for the teacher

☒ total group activity
☐ individual activity
☒ partner activity

Total Group Activity

Before beginning this activity, discuss the symbols for "less than" ($<$) and "greater than" ($>$). Write the numerals 1 to 16 on the chalkboard. Choose one of these numerals and write it on a slip of paper or on the chalkboard where it can't be seen until you are ready to give the answer.

Tell the students that you have selected one of the numerals. They are to try to discover it by asking "greater than/less than" questions. Record their questions and your responses in code on the chalkboard. For example:

"Is it less than 8?" "Yes, my number is less than 8." ☐ < 8

"Is it greater than 4?" "Yes, it is greater than 4." ☐> 4

As you answer each of their questions, cross off the numerals eliminated:

~~1~~   ~~2~~   ~~3~~   ~~4~~   5   6   7   ~~8~~   ~~9~~   ~~10~~   ~~11~~   ~~12~~   ~~13~~   ~~14~~   ~~15~~   ~~16~~

Encourage the students to eliminate as many numbers as possible with each question. When they understand the concept, write the numerals 1 to 8 on the chalkboard and tell them it is possible to discover the answer within four questions. Later return to numerals 1 to 16 and challenge them to find the answer within five questions.

As their confidence grows, select a larger range of numbers. Eventually eliminate writing the numerals on the chalkboard and write only the "greater than/less than" responses. After each response, ask the student, "What can you tell about my number now?" For example: ☐ > 43 ☐ < 75 "Your number is greater than 43 and it is less than 75." Or, "Your number is somewhere between 43 and 75."

Partner Adaptation

Materials needed
paper for each student
pencil for each student

The partners decide upon the range of numbers they will use; for example, numbers between 0 and 100. The first player secretly writes a numeral on a piece of paper. The other student tries to determine the number by asking "greater than/less than" questions. As each question is asked, a tally mark is made. When the number has been guessed, the students reverse roles. The first person with twenty-five tally marks loses.

To make this a silent activity, have the students *write* their questions and responses rather than say them aloud.

56   I'M THINKING OF A FRACTION

Materials needed
chalkboard
chalk
eraser

☒ total group activity
☐ individual activity
☐ partner activity

Total Group Activity

For this activity students need to understand that the bottom number of a fraction (denominator) tells how many equal parts something has been divided into, and that the top number (numerator) indicates how many parts we are thinking about.

Write the following fractions on the chalkboard:

3/7   3/8   4/7   8/3   2/3

Ask questions such as the following:

1. "I'm thinking of a fraction. The whole has been divided into 7 equal parts, and I am thinking about 4 of the parts. What number am I thinking about?" **(4/7)**

2. "I'm thinking of a fraction. The whole has been divided into 8 equal parts. I am thinking about 3 of these parts. What number am I thinking about?" **(3/8)**

3. "I'm thinking of a fraction. There are two whole circles. Each has been divided into 4 equal pieces. I'm thinking about 7 of these pieces. What number am I thinking about? **(7/4)**
   Who can draw a picture showing this answer?

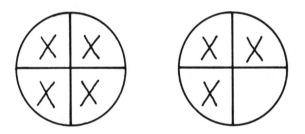

What's another way to say the same thing? **(1¾)**

After asking several questions like these, erase the numbers on the chalkboard, write a new group of fractions, and continue questioning.

Once students are familiar with the type of questions that can be asked, have them assume the role of "questioner." The student who gives the correct answer may ask the next question.

Follow-Up Activity

Materials needed
½ sheet of lined paper for each student
pencil for each student

Review this activity at a later time, having students write their answers on half sheets of lined paper.

57   SO YOU THINK YOU'RE BIGGER!

Materials needed
chalkboard
chalk
eraser

☒   total group activity
☐   individual activity
☐   partner activity

Total Group Activity

Review fractions with the students, making certain they understand that the bottom number of a fraction, the denominator, tells how many equal parts something has been divided into.

Draw the following illustration on the chalkboard, explaining that the *larger* the bottom number, the *smaller* the size of the fraction, for example, as the whole is divided into more equal pieces, each piece becomes smaller.

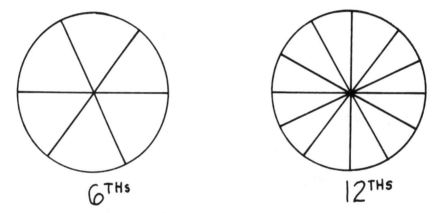

Have them study the illustration. Then ask which fraction is larger, ⅙ or 1/12. (**⅙**)

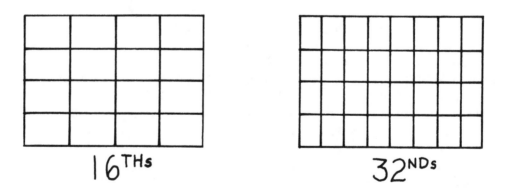

Draw two rectangles and divide them into 1/16ths and 1/32nds. Ask, "Which is larger, 1/16 or 1/32?" (**1/16**)
Through questioning of this type, help them discover that if fractions have the same number on top (numerator), then the *larger* the *bottom* number, the *smaller the size of the fraction*.

Read the following pairs of fractions twice slowly. The students are to decide which of each pair is larger. If the first fraction is larger they should hold up one finger. If the second fraction is larger they should hold up two fingers.

Remind them to think before responding. To provide ample thinking time, after you read the fractions hold up your opened hand and silently count to five. They should indicate their answers when you close your fist.

Variation: The same kind of activity can be applied to decimals. For example:

.1 ($1/10$) is larger than .01 ($1/100$)
.001 ($1/1000$) is smaller than .01 ($1/100$)

Which Is Larger, the First Fraction or the Second?

1. $1/5$ or $1/10$ **(first)**
2. $1/45$ or $1/30$ **(second)**
3. $4/9$ or $4/7$ **(second)**
4. $2/5$ or $2/8$ **(first)**
5. $3/16$ or $3/4$ **(second)**
6. $4/7$ or $4/11$ **(first)**
7. $2/15$ or $2/13$ **(second))**
8. $5/16$ or $5/24$ **(first)**
9. $3/8$ or $3/16$ **(first)**
10. $1/16$ or $1/64$ **(first)**
11. $6/15$ or $6/11$ **(second)**
12. $4/13$ or $4/15$ **(first)**
13. $3/10$ or $3/20$ **(first)**
14. $2/7$ or $2/11$ **(first)**
15. $6/15$ or $6/7$ **(second)**
16. $4/9$ or $4/19$ **(first)**
17. $1/26$ or $1/24$ **(second)**
18. $3/8$ or $3/7$ **(second)**
19. $5/14$ or $5/32$ **(first))**
20. $2/5$ or $2/7$ **(first)**

58   LOWEST COMMON DENOMINATOR CHALLENGE

Materials needed
chalkboard
chalk
eraser
½ sheet of paper for each student
pencil for each student
Optional: clock *or* timer

☒ total group activity
☐ individual activity
☐ partner activity

Total Group Activity

Write two fractions from the following list on the chalkboard and review the process of finding the lowest common denominator. When students understand the concept, divide the class into two teams and number the players. Have each student use a pencil and a half sheet of paper.

Write two of the following fractions on the chalkboard. Player 1 on Team A and player 1 on Team B compete to be the first to write the lowest common denominator on their papers. The players indicate they are finished by raising their pencils in the air.

The player whose pencil was raised first reads his or her answer. If it is correct, that team receives one point. If the answer is incorrect, the team loses one point and the other player's answer is read. One point is awarded if it is correct. No points are received or lost if it is incorrect.

Play continues in the same manner, with Player 2 on Team A and Player 2 on Team B competing. If a reasonable length of time elapses and players have not held their pencils in the air, give the answer and write two new fractions on the chalkboard for the next players on the teams.

The game ends when all students have had a turn, or at the end of a designated time period. The team with the most points wins.

What Is the Lowest Common Denominator?

1. $\frac{5}{6}$	$\frac{7}{18}$	**(18)**	13. $\frac{5}{12}$	$\frac{2}{5}$	**(60)**	25. $\frac{3}{4}$	$\frac{15}{32}$	**(32)**
2. $\frac{2}{3}$	$\frac{1}{4}$	**(12)**	14. $\frac{3}{4}$	$\frac{5}{6}$	**(12)**	26. $\frac{3}{4}$	$\frac{5}{6}$	**(12)**
3. $\frac{3}{4}$	$\frac{11}{32}$	**(32)**	15. $\frac{3}{4}$	$\frac{7}{9}$	**(36)**	27. $\frac{5}{6}$	$\frac{3}{8}$	**(24)**
4. $\frac{3}{4}$	$\frac{1}{6}$	**(12)**	16. $\frac{2}{3}$	$\frac{4}{15}$	**(15)**	28. $\frac{5}{9}$	$\frac{3}{4}$	**(36)**
5. $\frac{7}{8}$	$\frac{2}{5}$	**(40)**	17. $\frac{7}{9}$	$\frac{1}{6}$	**(18)**	29. $\frac{3}{8}$	$\frac{7}{10}$	**(40)**
6. $\frac{9}{24}$	$\frac{5}{8}$	**(24)**	18. $\frac{5}{8}$	$\frac{1}{6}$	**(24)**	30. $\frac{7}{12}$	$\frac{3}{4}$	**(12)**
7. $\frac{5}{8}$	$\frac{5}{6}$	**(24)**	19. $\frac{5}{6}$	$\frac{3}{7}$	**(42)**	31. $\frac{5}{12}$	$\frac{5}{8}$	**(24)**
8. $\frac{7}{12}$	$\frac{3}{4}$	**(12)**	20. $\frac{1}{6}$	$\frac{2}{15}$	**(30)**	32. $\frac{1}{2}$	$\frac{2}{9}$	**(18)**
9 $\frac{3}{5}$	$\frac{1}{4}$	**(20)**	21. $\frac{17}{20}$	$\frac{3}{5}$	**(20)**	33. $\frac{2}{15}$	$\frac{1}{6}$	**(30)**
10. $\frac{3}{4}$	$\frac{7}{10}$	**(20)**	22. $\frac{7}{9}$	$\frac{3}{4}$	**(36)**	34. $\frac{1}{8}$	$\frac{5}{6}$	**(24)**
11. $\frac{1}{2}$	$\frac{15}{16}$	**(16)**	23. $\frac{5}{6}$	$\frac{4}{9}$	**(18)**	35. $\frac{5}{6}$	$\frac{7}{18}$	**(18)**
12. $\frac{3}{10}$	$\frac{5}{8}$	**(40)**	24. $\frac{4}{5}$	$\frac{1}{4}$	**(20)**			

59   FORWARD—BACKWARD

Materials needed
½ sheet of lined paper for each student
pencil for each student

☒   total group activity
☐   individual activity
☐   partner activity

Total Group Activity

An important part of good problem-solving technique is following directions accurately. This activity gives practice in this skill.

As a warm-up activity, pick a number and ask students to count silently forward or backward by a specified amount. Ask a volunteer for the answer. For example:

56—Count forward 3.   **(59)**

75—Count backward 4.   **(71)**

78—Count forward 5.   **(83)**

62—Count backward 3.   **(59)**

When students are confident of the process, have them each use a half sheet of lined paper and instruct them as follows.

Jimmy
47
50
45
52
42
ⓐ39

1. Write 47 at the top of your paper. **(47)**

2. Count forward 3, skip a line on your paper, and write the new number. **(50)** *(Ask what number they wrote to make certain they understand the directions.)*

3. Count backward 5, skip a line, and write your new number. **(45)**

4. Count forward 7, skip a line, and write the number. **(52)**

5. Count backward 10, skip a line, and write the number. **(42)**

6. Count backward 3, skip a line, and write the number. **(39)**

7. Circle your last number.

Ask for their final number. If you get several different responses, have the students vote on which number they think is correct. Then give the answer.

60   MORE OR LESS?

Materials needed
none
Optional: 1 copy of students' math book

☒ total group activity
☐ individual activity
☐ partner activity

Total Group Activity

Use either the sample story problems below or those from the students' math book, or create your own. After reading each problem ask, "Will the answer be *more* or *less* than the first number in the problem?" "How do you know?" For example:

Betty bought 15 tickets for the school fair. She used 3 of them. How many does she have left?

Student response: "The answer will be less than 15, because she's used some of her tickets. She couldn't still have the same number she started with."

After four or five sample problems, have a student volunteer to tell a story problem and ask the "more than/less than" questions. The child who answers correctly either tells the next story problem or chooses another student storyteller.

Is the Answer More Than or Less Than the First Number?

1. There used to be 30 children in our classroom. Three students moved away. How many students are in our class now? **(Answer will be less than 30.)**

2. Tom and Jake went fishing. Tom caught 7 fish and Jake caught 5. How many did the two boys catch? **(Answer will be more than 7.)**

3. There are 12 napkins in a package. How many napkins would there be in 3 packages? **(Answer will be more than 12.)**

4. Mother is packing 4 lunches. She wants to put 3 small cookies in each lunch. How many cookies does she need? **(Answer will be more than 4.)**

5. The Browns are getting ready to go on vacation. They plan to drive 200 miles each day. How many miles will they travel in 4 days? **(Answer will be more than 200.)**

61   HERE'S THE NUMBER SENTENCE— YOU TELL ME THE STORY

Materials needed
chalkboard
chalk
eraser

☒ total group activity
☐ individual activity
☐ partner activity

Total Group Activity

Write a number sentence on the chalkboard. For example:

$$\square + 7 = 15$$

Call on a volunteer to tell a story that goes with the number sentence.

Billy and I went fishing this afternoon. I didn't count how many fish I caught, but Billy knows he caught 7. All together we have 15. How many fish did I catch? **(8)**

After several stories have been told about one number sentence, erase it and write a new one. For variety, periodically replace the place-holder box with either the letter X or N, explaining that these can be used interchangeably to indicate a missing number.

Here's the Number Sentence—You Tell Me the Story

(1) $6 + 3 = \square$ **(9)**

(2) $8 + \square = 12$ **(4)**

(3) $13 - 8 = \square$ **(5)**

(4) $12 - \square = 7$ **(5)**

(5) $\square - 4 = 9$ **(13)**

(6) $3 \times 6 = \square$ **(18)**

(7) $\square \times 7 = 28$ **(4)**

(8) $4 \times \square = 36$ **(9)**

(9) $15 \div 3 = \square$ **(5)**

(10) $24 \div \square = 6$ **(4)**

(11) $\square \div 7 = 3$ **(21)**

(Be certain that students specify that the objects are divided into *equal* groups. Dividing 15 into 3 groups could mean groups of 8, 5, and 2!)

62   SAY IT ANOTHER WAY

Materials needed
none
Optional: 1 copy of students' math book

[X] total group activity
[ ] individual activity
[ ] partner activity

Total Group Activity

Use the sample story problems below or read one from the students' math book. For example:

There are 27 apples on our tree and 39 apples on our neighbor's tree. How many more apples are there on our neighbor's tree?

Have a student rephrase the problem, using his or her *own words* to explain what information is to be found.

"There are apples on two trees and you want me to find out how many more apples there are on your neighbor's tree."

Next have the student explain how to solve the problem *without saying any numbers*.

"I'd subtract the number of apples on your tree from the number of apples on your neighbor's tree to find out how many more apples your neighbor has."

After a problem has been discussed by one student, ask if anyone has a different way to solve the problem. Stress that there may be more than one way to find the answer.

After going over several examples, call on a student volunteer to tell a story problem and elicit the problem-solving technique in the same way. The child who answers correctly either tells the next story or calls on another student storyteller.

Story Problems

1. Dan had 6 tropical fish. His brother bought 3 fish at the pet store. How many fish do they have now? **(9)**

2. Kelly is 8 years old and her little sister is 5 years old. How much older is Kelly? **(3 years)**

3. Jane has a collection of 14 stuffed animals. Her friend Carol has 23. How many more stuffed animals does Carol have? **(9)**

4. Rachel has 35 baseball cards. Kevin has 49. How many cards do they have altogether? **(84)**

5. Jamie has collected 42 soft drink bottles to take to the grocery store. He put 6 bottles in each carton. How many cartons did he fill? **(7)**

6. Mr. Fletcher has 35 desks in his classroom. He put 7 desks in each row. How many rows of desks are there? **(5)**

7. There are 12 pencils in a package. How many pencils are there in 6 packages? **(72)**

8. There are 24 hours in each day. How many hours are there in 7 days? **(168)**

9. Betty wants to read her library book in 10 days. There are 210 pages in the book. How many pages would she need to read each day? **(21)**

10. Karen sleeps 8 hours a night. How many hours does she sleep in 30 days? **(240)**

Variation

Materials needed
chalkboard
chalk
eraser
sheet of lined paper for each student
pencil for each student

Have each student write a story problem with its solution on a piece of lined paper. Have one student read his or her problem. As each key number is said, write it on the chalkboard as a reference for the class. The student should then reread the story problem as the rest of the class writes a number sentence and the solution. Discuss the answer and the process they used to find the answer. Stress that there are often several ways to solve a problem. Continue in the same manner, having other students volunteer to read their problems.

63   ROUNDING OFF

Materials needed

chalkboard
chalk
eraser
½ sheet of paper for each student
pencil for each student
Optional: clock *or* timer

Total Group Activity

Review rounding off numbers to the nearest ten, reminding students that numbers that end in five are generally rounded upward. Then review rounding off numbers to the nearest hundred and nearest thousand.

When students understand the concept, divide the class into two teams and number the players. Have each student use a pencil and a half sheet of paper.

Write a number from the following list on the chalkboard and announce how the number should be rounded (to the nearest ten, hundred, or thousand). Player 1 on Team A and Player 1 on Team B compete to be the first to have the answer written on paper. The players indicate they are finished by raising their pencils in the air.

The player whose pencil was raised first reads his or her answer. If it is correct, that team receives one point. If the answer is incorrect, the team loses one point and the other player's answer is read. One point is awarded if it is correct. No points are received or lost if it is incorrect.

Play continues in the same manner, with Player 2 on Team A and Player 2 on Team B competing. If players do not hold their pencils in the air by the count of ten, give the answer and write a new number on the chalkboard for the next players on the teams.

The game ends when all students have had a turn, or at the end of a designated time period. The team with the most points wins.

Round These Numbers

(1) 5647   Round to the nearest ten. **(5650)**

(2) 7284   Round to the nearest thousand. **(7000)**

(3) 8132   Round to the nearest ten. **(8130)**

(4) 3443   Round to the nearest hundred. **(3400)**

(5) 4786   Round to the nearest thousand. **(5000)**

(6) 8278   Round to the nearest ten. **(8280)**

(7) 3735   Round to the nearest thousand. **(4000)**

(8) 7129   Round to the nearest ten. **(7130)**

(9) 8471   Round to the nearest hundred. **(8500)**

(10) 8262   Round to the nearest hundred. **(8300)**

(11) 5448   Round to the nearest ten. **(5450)**

(12) 2687   Round to the nearest ten. **(2690)**

(13) 1326   Round to the nearest hundred. **(1300)**

(14) 7269   Round to the nearest thousand. **(7000)**

(15) 2775   Round to the nearest hundred. **(2800)**

64   IS IT LOGICAL?

Materials needed
chalkboard
chalk
eraser
½ sheet of lined paper for each student
pencil for each student
Optional: crayons

☒ total group activity
☐ individual activity
☐ partner activity

Total Group Activity

On the chalkboard write pairs of numbers to be added. For example: 37 + 63. Have the students mentally round off each number. Ask, "If I added these two numbers, would a logical answer be 90?" **(no)** Ask them to respond with yes or no or thumbs up or thumbs down.

Repeat this exercise until the students are confident of the process. Then have them number lined paper from one to ten and write yes or no responses to each problem on the following list. If time permits, give the answers and have the students correct their papers with crayons.

Estimate These Sums and Differences to the Nearest Ten

1. 42 + 39	(80)—**(yes)**	15. 87 − 39	(50)—**(yes)**
2. 26 + 45	(50)—**(no)**	16. 92 − 57	(40)—**(no)**
3. 39 + 18	(50)—**(no)**	17. 74 − 38	(30)—**(yes)**
4. 59 + 23	(80)—**(yes)**	18. 81 − 29	(50)—**(yes)**
5. 74 + 67	(140)—**(yes)**	19. 63 − 46	(30)—**(no)**
6. 83 + 49	(120)—**(no)**	20. 72 − 33	(50)—**(no)**
7. 67 + 68	(140)—**(yes)**	21. 91 − 49	(50)—**(no)**
8. 446 + 232	(680)—**(yes)**	22. 793 − 367	(430)—**(no)**
9. 334 + 229	(590)—**(no)**	23. 881 − 239	(640)—**(yes)**
10. 247 + 138	(370)—**(no)**	24. 587 − 232	(360)—**(yes)**
11. 372 + 521	(890)—**(yes)**	25. 674 − 459	(210)—**(yes)**
12. 123 + 739	(880)—**(no)**	26. 944 − 727	(200)—**(no)**
13. 354 + 228	(580)—**(yes)**	27. 486 − 213	(260)—**(no)**
14. 437 + 254	(690)—**(yes)**	28. 872 − 631	(240)—**(yes)**

Estimate These Sums and Differences to the Nearest Hundred

29. 498 + 264	(800)—**(yes)**	35. 774 + 921	(1700)—**(yes)**
30. 732 + 183	(800)—**(no)**	36. 784 − 429	(400)—**(yes)**
31. 479 + 183	(600)—**(no)**	37. 893 − 274	(600)—**(yes)**
32. 367 + 129	(500)—**(yes)**	38. 689 − 392	(400)—**(no)**
33. 381 + 268	(800)—**(no)**	39. 928 − 267	(600)—**(yes)**
34. 896 + 383	(1500)—**(no)**	40. 731 − 198	(600)—**(no)**

65   THE OLD SWITCHEROO

Materials needed
½ sheet of lined paper for each student
2 pieces of paper approximately 2″ x 2″ for each student
pencil for each student

☒ total group activity
☐ individual activity
☐ partner activity

Total Group Activity

Have each student use *two pieces* of paper approximately 2″ x 2″ and a half sheet of lined paper. Each student is to mark 6 dots on one of the small papers and 4 dots on the other.

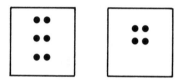

Have them write the numeral 6 on the first line of the lined paper, followed by a comma, the numeral 4, and another comma.

Ask them to add the dots, write the number after the last comma, and draw a box around the three numbers.

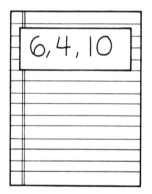

Ask if anyone can "see" an addition problem (**6 + 4 = 10** *or* **4 + 6 = 10**). (The 2″ square papers may help students visualize the problem.)

After the first problem has been answered, the students record it on their lined paper as shown here. Then challenge them to find another addition problem using these three numbers.

For subtraction, remind students that the largest number must be written first, followed by the smaller one. Ask if anyone can make up a subtraction problem using the three numbers. (It may help for students to *look at and say the total* on the 2″ square papers and then *actually pick up* the paper that has the number of dots that they are going to take away.) Follow the same procedure for the remaining subtraction problem. Both should be recorded on the students' papers.

Ask the students to add another dot on each of their small papers, for a total of 7 dots and 5 dots.

Have them skip two lines on their lined paper and write the new numbers and the total. The numbers should be separated by commas, and a box drawn around them.

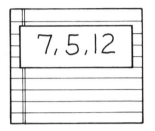

Proceed as above. After they record each set of four problems, continue the activity with the addition of another dot.

Follow-Up Activity

Materials needed
½ sheet of lined paper for each student
pencil for each student

Follow the above procedure, but have the students write the dots directly on their half sheets of lined paper. They should list the four possible problems beneath the illustration. In this way students work the same type of problems, but without the physical manipulation.

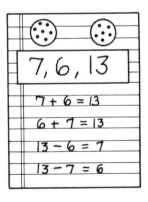

66   LISTEN AND DO

Materials needed
chalkboard
chalk
eraser
½ sheet of lined paper for each student
pencil for each student

☒ total group activity
☐ individual activity
☐ partner activity

Total Group Activity

In this activity students write two numbers and then find their sum or difference. A new number is written, then added to or subtracted from the previous answer. The activity continues in this manner.

Students enjoy volunteering the numbers, but it is necessary to establish parameters so that the problems are appropriate for their ability level. To do this, write two numbers on the chalkboard and ask students to name any number that is in between. Call on a student to say a number and have everyone write it on the top line of their paper. Have another student say a number, and instruct students to write it on the next line, directly beneath the first one. Indicate whether they should write a plus or a minus sign. Then have them solve the problem.

Ask for the answer. If some students have an incorrect answer, allow time for them to correct it. Continue having students write numbers directly beneath one another and discussing answers until they are confident about the procedure. Then omit discussing the answers until they get to the bottom of the page. Ask students for their final answer. If there is more than one response, have the class vote on which answer they think is correct. (This gives you an opportunity to determine how many did accurate calculations.) Then work through the computation on the board with the class.

$$
\begin{array}{r}
25 \\
+36 \\
\hline
{}^{5}\cancel{6}1 \\
-23 \\
\hline
38 \\
-17 \\
\hline
21 \\
+48 \\
\hline
69 \\
-35 \\
\hline
\textcircled{34}
\end{array}
$$

67   FIND MY NUMBERS

Materials needed
chalkboard
chalk
eraser

☒ total group activity
☒ individual activity
☐ partner activity

Total Group Activity

Write five different numbers on the chalkboard. For example: 13   4   8   5   10

Ask the students to solve the following problems:

1. The sum of which two numbers is 21?   **(13, 8)**
2. The difference between which two numbers is 8?   **(13, 5)**
3. The sum of which two numbers is 13?   **(8, 5)**
4. The difference between which two numbers is 6?   **(10, 4)**
5. The sum of which three numbers is 22?   **(10, 8, 4)**
6. Which numbers make a sum of 30?   **(13, 4, 8, 5)**

Erase the chalkboard then write five new numbers, continuing in the same manner using the problems below in Set A and Set B.

Adaptation for an Individual Student

Materials needed
paper (6″ x 9″ for class book)
pencil

On a piece of paper the student writes five numerals and a variety of questions like the ones above. The solution to each question is written on the back of the paper. When you have collected a sufficient number of these papers, they can be assembled into a class book of number puzzles for individual or whole class use.

Find My Numbers

Set A: 12   6   3   11   4

1. The sum of which two numbers is 16?   **(12, 4)**
2. The difference between which two numbers is 9?   **(12, 3)**
3. The sum of which two numbers is 17?   **(11, 6)**
4. The difference between which two numbers is 5?   **(11, 6)**
5. The sum of which three numbers is 20?   **(11, 3, 6)**
6. Which numbers make a sum of 13?   **(6, 4, 3)**

Set B: 9   14   2   7   5

1. The sum of which two numbers is 14?   **(9, 5)**
2. The difference between which two numbers is 9?   **(14, 5)**
3. The sum of which two numbers is 21?   **(14, 7)**
4. The difference between which two numbers is 4?   **(9, 5)**
5. The sum of which three numbers is 23?   **(14, 7, 2)**
6. Which numbers make a sum of 18?   **(9, 2, 7)**

68   SUM FUN

Materials needed
chalkboard
chalk
eraser
½ sheet of lined paper for each student
pencil for each student
Optional: ruler

☒   total group activity
☐   individual activity
☒   partner activity

Total Group Activity

Draw a three- or four-column grid on the chalkboard and write different numerals between 1 and 20 at the top of each column. Have the students copy the grid and numerals on lined paper.

Designate a numeral between 20 and 50 to be written at the top of the page. Challenge the students to determine how many different ways they can make this number using *only* the numerals in each column. Each numeral may be used a maximum of five times for any one sum. Each time a number is used, a check is placed in the appropriate column, but no more than five checks may be placed in any one space for the sum. An example is illustrated here.

27		
1	3	8
	√	√ √ √
√ √	√ √ √	√ √
√ √ √ √	√ √ √ √ √	√
√ √ √		√ √ √
√ √ √ √ √	√ √	√ √

Partner Adaptation (Grades 4–6)

Materials needed
paper
pencils
Optional: ruler
timer *or* clock

Each partner makes a three-column grid. One player names three numbers between 2 and 10. Both students write these in the columns at the top of their grids.

The other player names a number between 20 and 50 which is written at the very top of their papers. For the next five minutes, each student tries to find as many ways as possible to make the designated number. At the end of five minutes, the students check one another's papers. One point is awarded for each correct answer.

Students make a new grid and proceed as above. The first player with fifteen points wins.

69   START HERE—END THERE!

Materials needed
chalkboard
chalk
eraser
sheet of lined paper for each student
pencil for each student

☒ total group activity
☒ individual activity
☐ partner activity

Total Group Activity

Write two numbers on the chalkboard. For example:

8   27

Ask students to find at least three ways to get from the first number to the second number. They may use any combination of addition, subtraction, multiplication, and division to reach their goal. For example:

$$8 \times 4 - 5 = 27$$
$$8 \times 3 + 3 = 27$$
$$8 \times 2 + 20 - 9 = 27$$

Note that the computations must be done consecutively in these problems and one at a time.

Adaptation for an Individual Student

Materials needed
chalkboard
chalk
eraser
paper
pencil

Write several pairs of numbers on the chalkboard. Have the student write as many as possible to get from the first number of each pair to the second number.

70   BEAT MY SUM

Materials needed
chalkboard
chalk
eraser
½ sheet of lined paper for each student and the teacher
pencil for each student

☒ total group activity
☐ individual activity
☐ partner activity

Total Group Activity

On the chalkboard write the following:

$$\begin{array}{r} -\ -\ - \\ +\ -\ -\ - \\ \hline \end{array}$$

Tell students you are going to write six different numerals between 1 and 9 on a piece of paper and name them one at a time. The students are to try to make as large a sum as possible using only these numbers. As each number is called, a student comes to the chalkboard and writes it on any one of the lines. When all of the lines have been filled, the numbers are added.

$$\begin{array}{r} 1\ 1 \\ 2\ 1\ 9 \\ +\ 4\ 8\ 3 \\ \hline 7\ 0\ 2 \end{array}$$

Look at the sum and ask if there is any way it could have been made larger. Help the students discover that the lower numbers are best placed in the ones column and the higher numbers in the hundreds column in order to create the largest sum possible.

However, deciding where to place numbers is not as simple as it might sound, since not all numbers between 1 and 9 will be called. Give the following example:

$$\begin{array}{r} 5 \\ +\ 7\ 4\ 1 \\ \hline \end{array}$$

If a 6 is called for this problem, the player has to decide whether to write it in the ones column or in the hundred's column. The student knows a 9 has not been called yet, so he decides to write the 6 in the ones column and hopes a 9 is called for the last number. Unfortunately, a 2 is called, resulting in the player having a lower total sum than he would have had if he had transposed the 6 and 2.

When students understand the strategies (and luck) involved, have them draw the original diagram on lined paper. While they are doing this, write a new group of six different numerals between 1 and 9 on your paper.

Call out your numbers, one at a time, having the students write each numeral on one of their lines. When all six have been named, ask them to add the numbers. Students should volunteer their sums to determine who has the highest total.

If time permits, repeat the game with a student leader.

71   ZERO WINS

Materials needed
chalkboard
chalk
eraser

☒   total group activity
☐   individual activity
☒   partner activity

Total Group Activity

Divide the class into two teams. Explain that each team will start with 100 points and the first team to get exactly to zero wins.

Have the teams choose which one goes first by any method you wish. The team that begins the game may subtract up to 10 points on its first move. Play then goes to the next team, who may subtract up to 10 points more than the amount subtracted by the first team on its move or any amount of points below that number if they wish. For example, if Team A had just subtracted 8, Team B could subtract 18 points (8 + 10) or fewer.

Alternate calling on different members of each team to give numbers. Encourage the students to develop game strategies. for example, while a high number might be subtracted, it gives the opposing team the opportunity to subtract an even higher number on their turn. For example:

TEAM A	TEAM B
100	100
− 1	− 11
99	89
− 21	− 3
78	86
− 13	− 23
65	63
− 33	− 10
32	53
− 20	− 30
12	23
− 12	
0—WINNER	

Partner Adaptation

Materials needed
paper
pencils

Students follow the above rules. The first player to reach zero receives one point. Five points wins the game.

72   SO YOU LIKE 3's

Materials needed
chalkboard
chalk
eraser
sheet of lined paper for each student
pencil for each student

Total Group Activity

This activity provides practice in addition.

On the chalkboard write the numerals 1 to 9 in a horizontal line and have the students copy them on their papers. Ask them to write the same lines of numerals two more times, placing them beneath those in the first line.

```
1  2  3  4  5  6  7  8  9
1  2  3  4  5  6  7  8  9
1  2  3  4  5  6  7  8  9
```

For the fourth, fifth, and sixth lines, ask the students to write the numerals 9 to 1 in descending order, writing each beneath the numerals in the lines above.

```
1  2  3  4  5  6  7  8  9
1  2  3  4  5  6  7  8  9
1  2  3  4  5  6  7  8  9
9  8  7  6  5  4  3  2  1
9  8  7  6  5  4  3  2  1
9  8  7  6  5  4  3  2  1
```

As a final step, have them write a 3 under the right-hand column and find the sum of all the numbers. **(To their amazement they'll discover the answer contains nothing but 3's!)**

```
    123456789
    123456789
    123456789
    987654321
    987654321
    987654321
+           3
  3,333,333,333
```

73   PICK A SECRET NUMBER

Materials needed
½ sheet of paper for each student
pencil for each student

Total Group Activity

This activity provides practice in addition.
One at a time, read the following directions to the students and ask them to calculate them on paper.

1. Choose a secret number between 10 and 100.
2. Add 95.
3. Cross off the numeral in the hundred's place.
4. Add the digit you crossed off.
5. Add 4.
6. The resulting number should be your original secret number.

$$\begin{array}{r} 93 \\ +95 \\ \hline \cancel{1}88 \\ +\ \ 1 \\ \hline 89 \\ +\ \ 4 \\ \hline 93 \end{array}$$

74   MAGIC 1089 and 198

Materials needed
½ sheet of paper for each student
pencil for each student

[X]   total group activity
[ ]   individual activity
[ ]   partner activity

Total Group Activity

This activity provides practice in addition and subtraction.

Ask the students to choose any three-digit number. Before they follow a series of instructions, tell them that you already know their final answer if they calculate correctly (**1089** *or* **198**).

Read the following directions to the students.

1. Write a three-digit number.
2. Below it write the number in reverse order.
3. Subtract the smaller number from the larger number.
4. Below it write the new number in reverse order.
5. Add the last two numbers.

$$\begin{array}{r} 684 \\ -486 \\ \hline 198 \\ +891 \\ \hline 1089 \end{array}$$

(If all calculations are correct, the answer will be 1089. The only exception to this rule occurs if there is a difference of 1 between the first digit and last digit of the initial number, for example 6̲37̲ or 9̲38̲. In this case the answer will be 198.)

$$\begin{array}{r} 938 \\ -839 \\ \hline 99 \\ +\ 99 \\ \hline 198 \end{array}$$

75   IT CAN'T BE 7!

Materials needed
½ sheet of paper for each student
pencil for each student

☒ total group activity
☐ individual activity
☐ partner activity

Total Group Activity

This activity provides practice in addition, subtraction, and division.

Students choose a number with any amount of digits. Before you begin the activity, tell them that you already know that their final answer will be 7, provided they calculate correctly.

Read the following directions to the students.

1. Write a number.	155
2. Add 9.	+ 9
	164
3. Double the new number.	+164
	328
4. Subtract 4.	− 4
5. Divide the new number by 2.	2⟌324
	162
6. Subtract the number you originally chose.	−155
(With no errors, 7 is the answer.)	7

Variation: Instead of adding 9 in step 2, substitute "Add 7." The answer will always be 5.

76   I'VE GOT YOUR NUMBER!

Materials needed
½ sheet of paper for each student
pencil for each student

Total Group Activity

This activity provides practice in addition and multiplication.

Have the students follow these directions for two different "magic" tricks with one-digit and two-digit numbers.

A. ONE-DIGIT NUMBERS:

1. Choose a secret number between 1 and 9, and write it on your paper.

2. Multiply your number by 3.

3. Add 2.

4. Multiply the new number by 3.

5. Add your original number.

6. If your calculations are correct, your current number should end with a 6. Cross off the 6.

7. What remains should be your secret number.

$$
\begin{array}{r}
8 \\
\times\ 3 \\
\hline
24 \\
+\ 2 \\
\hline
26 \\
\times\ 3 \\
\hline
78 \\
+\ 8 \\
\hline
8\cancel{6}
\end{array}
$$

B. TWO-DIGIT NUMBERS:

1. Choose a secret two-digit number.

2. Multiply your number by 3.

3. Add 2.

4. Multiply the new number by 3.
5. Add your original two-digit number.

6. Cross off the 6.

7. What remains should be your secret number.

$$
\begin{array}{r}
47 \\
\times\ 3 \\
\hline
141 \\
+\ 2 \\
\hline
143 \\
\times\ 3 \\
\hline
429 \\
+\ 47 \\
\hline
47\cancel{6}
\end{array}
$$

77   I KNOW YOUR SECRET NUMBER!

Materials needed
½ sheet of paper for each student
pencil for each student

☒ total group activity
☐ individual activity
☐ partner activity

Total Group Activity

This activity provides practice in addition, subtraction, and multiplication by 2, 5, and 10.
Read the following directions to the students.

1. Select a secret number between 1 and 99 and write it on your paper.

$$54$$

2. Multiply the number by 2.

$$\begin{array}{r} \times\ \ 2 \\ \hline 108 \end{array}$$

3. Add 35.

$$\begin{array}{r} +\ \ 35 \\ \hline 143 \end{array}$$

4. Multiply your new number by 5.

$$\begin{array}{r} \times\ \ 5 \\ \hline 715 \end{array}$$

5. Subtract 155.

$$\begin{array}{r} -\ 155 \\ \hline 560 \end{array}$$

6. Multiply by 10.

$$\begin{array}{r} \times\ 10 \\ \hline 5600 \end{array}$$

7. Subtract 200.

$$\begin{array}{r} -\ 200 \\ \hline \end{array}$$

8. Cross off the last two digits, and the remaining number should be your original number!

$$54\cancel{00}$$

Variation: Challenge students to discover if the trick works when the secret number is larger than 99 **(yes)**.

78   HOCUS POCUS—I KNOW YOUR AGE!

Materials needed
½ sheet of paper for each student
pencil for each student

Total Group Activity

This activity provides practice in addition, and multiplication and division by 3.
Tell students that you can guess someone's age with this "magic trick."
Read the following directions to the students.

1. Write your age on a piece of paper, but don't show it to me.

2. Multiply your age by 3.

3. Add 12.

4. Divide by 3.

5. Add 93.
6. Tell me your answer, and I'll tell you how old you are. **(To determine the age, drop the first digit in the answer and add 3 to the remaining number.)**

$$12$$
$$\times\ 3$$
$$36$$
$$+\ 12$$

$$3\overline{)4'8}$$
$$16$$
$$+\ 93$$
$$109$$

$$\cancel{1}09$$
$$+\ \ 3$$
$$12$$

Since most of the students in the class are the same age, after one person has given the answer, ask how many others have the same answer. Then ask for any different answers and "reveal" the ages.

79   NOW I KNOW YOUR BIRTHDAY!

Materials needed
½ sheet of paper for each student and the teacher
pencil for each student

☒   total group activity
☐   individual activity
☐   partner activity

Total Group Activity

This activity provides practice in addition, subtraction, and multiplication.

Tell the students that you are going to use this "magic trick" to find out their birthdays. Before beginning, make certain they know the numerical equivalent for each month; 1 for January, 2 for February, and so on.

Read the following directions to the student. (In this example the birthday is October 31.)

1. In what month were you born? Write the number that stands for that month. For instance, if you were born in October, write 10.

$$10$$

2. Double the number.

$$\begin{array}{r} + \quad 10 \\ \hline 20 \end{array}$$

3. Add 6.

$$\begin{array}{r} + \quad 6 \\ \hline 26 \end{array}$$

4. Multiply your new number by 50.

$$\begin{array}{r} \times \quad 50 \\ \hline 1300 \end{array}$$

5. Add the day of your birth. For instance, if you were born on October 31, add 31.

$$\begin{array}{r} + \quad 31 \\ \hline 1331 \end{array}$$

6. Subtract 365.

$$\begin{array}{r} - \quad 365 \\ \hline 966 \end{array}$$

7. Tell me your answer and I'll tell you your birthday! **(To determine the birthday, write down the answer and secretly add 65. To divide it into a numerically written date, make a slash between the second and third digits from the right (between the tens and hundreds) and announce the student's birthday.)**

$$\begin{array}{r} + \quad 65 \\ \hline 10/31 \ \text{(Oct. 31)} \end{array}$$

80   SUM MAGIC

Materials needed
chalkboard
chalk
eraser
½ sheet of lined paper for each student
pencil for each student

☒ total group activity
☐ individual activity
☐ partner activity

Total Group Activity

This "magic trick" was discovered in Italy in the early 1200s by a mathematician named Fibonacci. It provides practice in addition and multiplication.

Have the students follow these directions:

1. One student names two numbers between 1 and 9. Write these on the chalkboard for all students to copy on their papers.
2. The students add the two numbers. The sum is written on the chalkboard and on their papers.
3. Point to the *last* two numbers (**7 and 11 in the example**) and ask the students to add these numbers (**18**). The answer should be written on their papers and on the chalkboard.
4. The last two numbers (**11 and 18 in the example**) are then added and written down below the others.
5. Continue in this manner, adding the last two numbers, until there are a total of ten numbers. Then ask the students to find the sum of all of these numbers.
6. Have the students locate the *seventh* number in the column and multiply it by 11. This number is the same as the sum of all ten numbers!

```
  4 ⎫
  7 ⎬
 11 ⎭
 18
 29
 47
 76 ────▶   76
123        × 11
199        ────
322          76
836          76
           ────
             836
```

Variation: Follow the same procedures but have the students start with two two-digit numbers.

81 BACK TO SQUARE ONE

Materials needed
chalkboard
chalk
eraser
½ sheet of paper for each student and the teacher
pencil for each student

☒ total group activity
☐ individual activity
☐ partner activity

Total Group Activity

This pair of tricks will unknowingly give students practice in dividing by 6 and 8, and also in adding, subtracting, and multiplying.

Read the following directions, having the students calculate on paper. Then teach them how the trick works.

1. Pick a number and write it on your paper.   562

2. Add 6. $\begin{array}{r} +\ \ \ 6 \\ \hline 568 \end{array}$

3. Multiply your new number by 4. $\begin{array}{r} \times\ \ \ 4 \\ \hline 2272 \end{array}$

4. Add 7. $\begin{array}{r} +\ \ \ 7 \\ \hline 2279 \end{array}$

5. Multiply by 2. $\begin{array}{r} \times\ \ \ 2 \\ \hline 4558 \end{array}$

6. Subtract 62. $\begin{array}{r} -\ \ 62 \\ \hline 4496 \end{array}$

7. Tell me your answer and I will tell you your original number. **(Write a student's answer on paper and divide by 8. This will give you the student's original number.)** $4496 \div 8 = 562$

After "discovering" several students' numbers, write the steps on the chalkboard in abbreviated form, as shown here. Encourage students to copy the directions and perform the "magic trick" for their friends and family.

$+6$
$\times 4$
$+7$
$\times 2$
-62
Secretly $\div 8$

Variation: If you want the students to practice dividing by 6, use the following directions.

1. Pick a number and write it on your paper.   724

2. Add 5. $\begin{array}{r} +\ \ \ 5 \\ \hline 729 \end{array}$

3. Multiply your new number by 2. $\begin{array}{r} \times\ \ \ 2 \\ \hline 1458 \end{array}$

4. Add 9. $\begin{array}{r} +\ \ \ 9 \\ \hline 1467 \end{array}$

5. Multiply by 3. $\begin{array}{r} \times\ \ \ 3 \\ \hline 4401 \end{array}$

6. Subtract 57. $\begin{array}{r} -\ \ 57 \\ \hline 4344 \end{array}$

7. **(To determine the secret number, divide by 6.)** $4344 \div 6 = 724$

82   RATIO DETECTIVE

Materials needed
chalkboard
chalk
eraser
sheet of unlined paper for each student
pencil for each student

[X] total group activity
[ ] individual activity
[ ] partner activity

Total Group Activity

Each student selects two shapes from a selection of squares, circles, rectangles, and triangles and mentally chooses the ratio he or she would like to illustrate (2:1, 3:4, 2:5, and so on).

Next the student draws a picture of the ratio using the two chosen shapes. As a final step, the ratio is disguised by proportionally increasing the numbers of chosen shapes. For instance, in the example illustration here, the chosen shapes, square and circle, were used to illustrate the ratio 3:1 **(12:4)**.

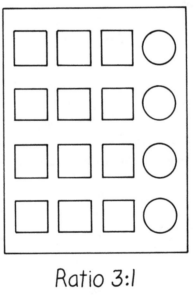

Ratio 3:1

Call on a student to give clues about his or her picture. Write the information on the chalkboard as it is given. The student then indicates the information the class is to discover.

In this example the clues might be:

"I drew 1 circle for every 3 squares. I have 4 circles. How many squares are there? **(12)**
or
"I have 12 squares and 4 circles. What ratio did I use? **(1 circle for every 3 squares)**
or
"I have a total of 16 shapes. I used a ratio of 1 circle for every 3 squares. How many circles and squares do I have?" **(4 circles and 12 squares)**

The student who gives the correct answer gets the opportunity to give clues about his or her picture.

83   1-2-3 TOTAL

Materials needed
paper
pencil

☐   total group activity
☐   individual activity
☒   partner activity

Partner Activity

This activity provides practice in addition.

Each player is to hold up any number of fingers on one hand or on both hands and guess the total number of fingers. Before they hold up fingers, each player secretly writes his or her estimate of the total, and then turns the paper over. Together they *silently* count, "1-2-3." On "3," both players hold up any number of fingers.

The total is determined and the player whose guess was closest receives one point. If both players wrote the same answer, both receive 1 point apiece. Likewise, if the difference between the total sum and each of the students' estimates is the same, they each receive 1 point. If a player guesses the *exact* score, 3 points are earned.

The first person with 15 points wins.

84   ROUND AND ROUND ADDITION

Materials needed
unlined paper
pencils
Optional: compass
Optional: ruler

☐   total group activity
☐   individual activity
☒   partner activity

Partner Activity

This activity provides practice in addition.

Have students draw one of the following diagrams at the top of a piece of paper. Younger students should use the diagram with fewer numbers. Below the diagram a column for each partner is drawn with their names heading the columns.

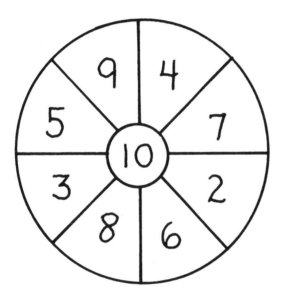
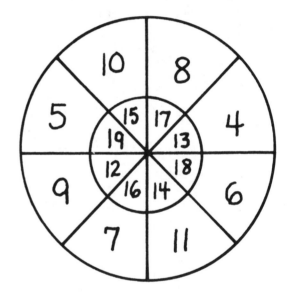

The partners decide who goes first and the diagram is placed in front of that person. This player then looks up at the ceiling and holds a pencil with the eraser end touching his or her nose. While continuing to look at the ceiling, the student puts the pencil point on the paper. The section of the diagram in which the pencil point lands indicates the number of points awarded to the student. He or she then writes the score in the appropriate column on the bottom half of the paper. If the pencil point doesn't land on a section of the diagram, the player repeats the procedure until successful.

The other student follows the above procedure. As the game progresses, each score is added to the previous score in the player's column. If students use the diagram with higher numbers, the first person to receive 100 points wins. If the smaller diagram is used, the first person to receive 50 points wins.

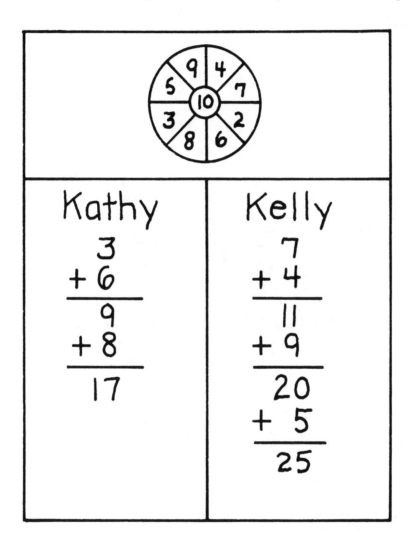

85   THE BOTTOM LINE IS ZERO

Materials needed
lined paper
pencils

☒ total group activity
☒ individual activity
☐ partner activity

Individual Activity

This activity provides practice in subtraction.

The student draws three vertical lines on a piece of paper, dividing it into four columns. Any number is written at the top of each column.

15	19	14	12
4	5	2	

The difference between the first two numbers (15 and 19 in the example) is written in the first column, the difference between the second and third numbers (19 and 14) in the second column, and the difference between the third and fourth numbers in the third column. The difference between the numbers in the first and last column (15 and 12 here) is written in the last column.

15	19	14	12
4	5	2	3

The same procedure is followed until there is an entire line of zeros across all columns.

15	19	14	12
4	5	2	3
1	3	1	1
2	2	0	0
0	2	0	2
2	2	2	2
0	0	0	0

Total Group Adaptation

Materials needed

chalkboard	*or*	sheet of lined paper for each student
chalk		pencil for each student
eraser		

Follow the above procedures but write the numbers on the chalkboard and have students work together, step by step, mentally doing the calculations and indicating the answers to be written on the chalkboard. Or have the students use lined paper. Tell them the numbers to write at the top of each column, and have them work the puzzle independently.

If time permits, work a second puzzle with a student providing the numbers at the column tops.

86   DIGIT DIVERSITY

Materials needed
paper
pencil

Individual Activity

This activity provides practice in addition, subtraction, and multiplication.

Challenge a student to see how many addition, subtraction, and multiplication problems can be created without repeating a digit within any specific problem. For example:

$$
\begin{array}{r}
28 \\
\times\ 7 \\
\hline
196
\end{array}
\qquad\qquad
\begin{array}{r}
37 \\
+28 \\
\hline
65
\end{array}
\qquad\qquad
\begin{array}{r}
93 \\
-52 \\
\hline
41
\end{array}
$$

(uses the digits 1, 2, 6, 7, 8, 9)   (uses the digits 2, 3, 5, 6, 7, 8)   (uses the digits 1, 2, 3, 4, 5, 9)

Variation: Have the student try to discover problems and their answers composed only of *sequential* digits. For example:

$$
\begin{array}{r}
47 \\
+\ 6 \\
\hline
53
\end{array}
\qquad\qquad
\begin{array}{r}
63 \\
+\ 42 \\
\hline
105
\end{array}
$$

(uses 3, 4, 5, 6, 7)   (uses 0, 1, 2, 3, 4, 5, 6)

87 NUMBER SENTENCE CODES

Materials needed
paper (6″ x 9″ for class book)
pencil

☐ total group activity
☒ individual activity
☐ partner activity

Individual Activity

This activity provides practice in addition, subtraction, multiplication, and division.

In this activity the student invents his or her own math code and writes it along the left-hand side of a piece of paper. Next to the code he or she writes a secret message or saying using a *math equation* for each letter. Collect completed papers and assemble them into a code puzzle book to be enjoyed by the class as individuals or as a group. One example is shown here.

A	3
B	15
C	2
D	32
E	5
F	8
G	9
H	24
I	45
J	10
K	19
L	14
M	26
N	4
O	50
P	28
Q	12
R	40
S	21
T	6
U	49
V	18
W	35
X	16
Y	37
Z	7

$6 \times 4 =$ ___H___   (24)   H
$100 \div 2 =$ _____   (50)   O
$7 \times 5 =$ _____   (35)   W

$9 \div 3 =$ _____   (3)   A
$400 \div 10 =$ _____   (40)   R
$35 \div 7 =$ _____   (5)   E

$18 + 19 =$ _____   (37)   Y
$25 + 25 =$ _____   (50)   O
$100 - 51 =$ _____   (40)   U
          ?   ?

88   FRACTION PATHS

Materials needed
6″ x 9″ unlined paper
pen

☐ total group activity
☒ individual activity
☐ partner activity

Individual Activity

This activity provides practice in adding, subtracting, multiplying, and dividing fractions.

In this activity the student designs fraction path challenges for other students. The path is composed of stepping stones each labelled with a fraction and a symbol (× − + ÷).

The steps of the path are computed in sequence from beginning to end and the final answer is written on the reverse side of the paper. Collect several papers and staple them into class booklets for individual practice in computing fractions.

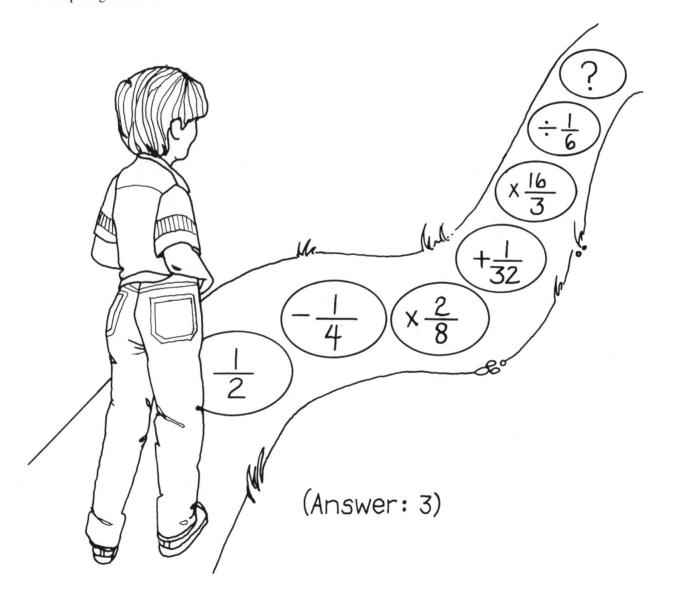

(Answer: 3)

89   DECIMAL DONUTS

Materials needed
6″ x 9″ unlined paper
pen
Optional: compass
Optional: ruler

☐   total group activity
☒   individual activity
☐   partner activity

Individual Activity

This activity provides practice in computing fractions.

Explain that a "decimal donut" is composed of a donut shape divided into any number of sections. Each section is labelled with a decimal or whole number and a symbol (× − + ÷). Sections are to be computed in sequence from beginning to end. The special feature of a "decimal donut" is that the beginning number and final number are identical. An example is shown here.

Challenge the student to write a "decimal donut" using as many fractions as possible. Collect several papers and staple them into class booklets for individual practice in computing fractions.

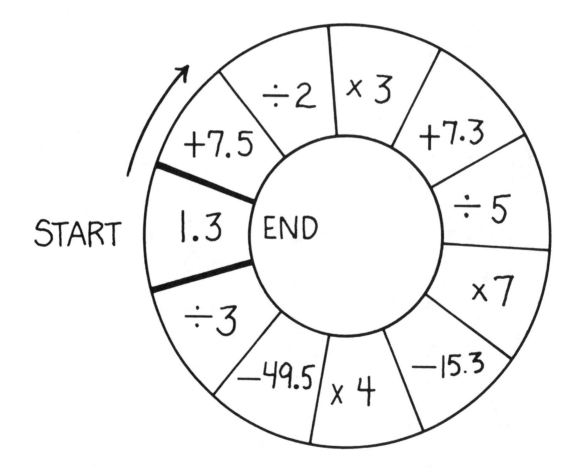

90   BRAINSTORMING RHYMES

Materials needed
none
Optional: chalkboard
Optional: chalk

☒ total group activity
☐ individual activity
☐ partner activity

Total Group Activity

Students are to name as many words as they can think of that rhyme with the word you give them from the following list. Tally each response on the board or hold up a finger for each word, and then count the total.

Explain to the students that if a word is said twice it will not be counted. This becomes a good listening and remembering activity if you ask the children to listen for duplicates. Periodically challenge them to see how many rhyming words they can name before one is repeated. As soon as there is a duplication, stop and count the total number of answers. Immediately follow with a new rhyming category, encouraging them to beat their previous record.

What Rhymes with—

1. pill	9. hide	17. sink	25. day
2. chin	10. night	18. rain	26. drum
3. stop	11. cake	19. bank	27. catch
4. cap	12. bug	20. gate	28. joke
5. ball	13. nail	21. round	29. sleep
6. race	14. feet	22. hair	30. glue
7. snow	15. flu	23. bark	31. peek
8. bed	16. camp	24. sip	32. made
			33. bead

91   MISMATCH RHYMES

Materials needed
none

☒ total group activity
☐ individual activity
☐ partner activity

Total Group Activity

Read the following groups of words to the students, explaining that one of the words in each group does not rhyme with the others. They should listen to all four words, then raise their hands if they locate the mismatched word. Call on a student to give the answer, then continue with the next group of words.

Which Is the Mismatch?

1. ball, call, saw, fall **(saw)**
2. snow, row, blow, blot **(blot)**
3. flu, blue, bloom, crew **(bloom)**
4. camp, lamb, lamp, damp **(lamb)**
5. sip, snap, snip, slip **(snap)**
6 day, gray, graze, way **(graze)**
7. beet, bead, seed, weed **(beet)**
8. black, slacks, sack, crack **(slacks)**
9. fast, fat, past, last **(fat)**
10. stall, tall, talk, hall **(talk)**
11. feet, foot, sleet, beet **(foot)**
12. hair, bear, tear, dared **(dared)**
13. true, moon, tune, spoon **(true)**
14. knife, ripe, type, pipe **(knife)**
15. bed, bet, dead, red **(bet)**
16. bath, path, match, math **(match)**
17. sing, sink, pink, rink **(sing)**
18. round, town, found, sound **(town)**
19. sleep, street, keep, leap **(street)**
20. end, blend, lent, send **(lent)**
21. bill, peel, will, spill **(peel)**
22. night, light, line, slight **(line)**
23. bank, bang, blank, plank **(bang)**
24. jump, crumb, lump, pump **(crumb)**
25. joke, throat, choke, soak **(throat)**
26. rain, drain, blame, train **(blame)**
27. lend, hen, pen, ten **(lend)**
28. cake, rake, rate, break **(rate)**

29. crate, gate, bait, bake   **(bake)**
30. bark, mark, dark, dart   **(dart)**
31. peek, bead, beak, creak   **(bead)**
32. feed, need, neat, seed   **(neat)**
33. stop, top, tap, hop   **(tap)**
34. beg, bug, dug, rug   **(beg)**
35. stop, stock, hop, drop   **(stock)**
36. drum, dump, dumb, crumb   **(dump)**
37. each, eat, teach, reach   **(eat)**
38. line, blind, nine, sign   **(blind)**
39. lap, cap, kept, clap   **(kept)**
40. race, taste, lace, face   **(taste)**
41. hide, ride, hike, side   **(hike)**
42. made, paid, stay, grade   **(stay)**
43. sick, stick, brick, picked   **(picked)**
44. catch, hat, hatch, match   **(hat)**
45. nail, stale, sailed, pail   **(sailed)**
46. born, torn, corn, storm   **(storm)**
47. fun, gum, gun, sun   **(gum)**
48. clock, dock, dot, block   **(dot)**
49. fat, cat, crack, bat   **(crack)**
50. plan, slam, swam, ham   **(plan)**

92   ASK-AND-ANSWER RHYMES

Materials needed
¼ sheet of paper for each student
pencil for each student

☒ total group activity
☐ individual activity
☐ partner activity

Total Group Activity

Each student thinks of a person, place, or object that has quite a few other words that rhyme with it. This word is written on his or her piece of paper. You should be the leader for the first round so that you can set the pattern for questions and answers. Begin the game by saying, "I'm thinking of a word that rhymes with *cat*.

A student might ask, "Is it an animal that eats cheese?" As the leader, you must determine the word the questioner has in mind and use it in your answer—"No, it is not a *rat*."

The next student might ask, "Is it an animal that sleeps in caves during the daytime?" to which you would reply, "No, it is not a *bat*."

Continue until one of the students guesses the word. That student begins the next round by saying, "I'm thinking of a word that rhymes with _____."

Tell students that if they cannot think of an indirect question, they may ask, "Does it start with ____?" (the name of a specific letter), but they should use this only as a last resort.

If someone asks a question and the leader cannot determine what word the questioner has in mind, ask the class if anyone knows what word the student is thinking of. The questioner then indicates whether or not it is the word he or she had in mind, and the game continues as before.

93   COMPOUND SPINOFF

Materials needed
dictionary

X   total group activity
☐   individual activity
☐   partner activity

Total Group Activity

Begin this activity by reviewing compound words (two words put together to make a new word) with students. Then name the first part of a compound word on the folowing list and ask the students to determine how the word ends. Explain that in many cases there will be more than one correct ending. When students are unable to think of additional compound words, give clues for some of the remaining words. For instance, if for *fire* they had named *fireman, fireplace,* and *fireplug,* you might ask, "Have you ever seen an insect on summer evenings that has a light that goes on and off?" **(firefly)** and "If something is made so that it will not catch on fire, we say it is _____." **(fireproof)**. You will find that clues of this type extend vocabulary and help develop listening and thinking skills.

Most likely, students will have problems differentiating between compound words and separate words. If a dispute arises, encourage upper-grade students to use a dictionary to prove their point. When working with younger students, you may want to make a list of words to be looked up at a later time.

What Word Can Form a Compound Word with—

1. flash	**(light)**		21. tooth	**(brush, paste, pick, ache)**
2. basket	**(ball)**		22. play	**(mate, ground, thing, pen, house, room)**
3. splash	**(down)**		23. dish	**(cloth, rag, towel, washer, pan, water)**
4. your	**(self)**			
5. cook	**(book)**		24. eye	**(lid, brow, lash, ball, glasses, sight, tooth, strain, dropper, sore, witness)**
6. cup	**(cake)**			
7. blind	**(fold)**			
8. lone	**(some)**			
9. summer	**(time)**		25. book	**(case, mark, mobile, worm, rack, shelf, stand, store, keeper)**
10. broom	**(stick)**			
11. finger	**(nail, print)**			
12. life	**(time, guard, saver, boat)**		26. rain	**(coat, drop, storm, bow, fall, spout)**
13. bean	**(bag, stalk)**			
14. rail	**(road, way)**		27. news	**(paper, boy, print, stand, letter, cast)**
15. steam	**(boat, ship)**			
16. class	**(mate, room)**		28. fire	**(man, place, house, works, cracker, wood, fly, plug, proof, boat, light, trap, side, arm, ball)**
17. farm	**(yard, house, hand)**			
18. sail	**(boat, fish)**			
19. candle	**(stick, holder, light)**			
20. mail	**(man, bag, box)**		29. door	**(bell, knob, way, step, mat, jamb, man)**

30. sand (box, paper, man, blast, bag, stone, piper, storm, bar)

31. any (one, body, how, thing, way, where, place)

32. sea (shore, coast, sick, food, weed, side, plane, going, worthy)

33. house (wife, work, top, coat, fly, boat, broken, keeper, hold)

34. some (time, where, body, how, one, thing, way, what, day, place)

35. hand (bag, writing, ball, made, spring, out, shake, clasp)

36. out (side, doors, field, run, line, grow, live, number, fit, come, standing, law, house, distance, put, wit, break, do, going, last, board, burst, cry)

37. day (break, dream, time, light)

38. rattle (snake, trap)

39. sun (shine, light, glasses, rise, set, up, down, burn, bathe, stroke, flower, beam, bonnet, day, dial, fish, spot, burst)

40. back (bone, door, stop, ground, hand, stroke, log, stage, spin, court, slide, lash, drop, fire, bite)

41. black (board, bird, berry, top, mail, out, smith, jack)

42. wind (mill, breaker, storm, burn, shield, pipe, bag)

43. sky (lark, cap, light, scraper, writing)

44. road (side, way, block, bed)

45. under (ground, way, clothes, wear, shirt, pants, line, side, stand, water, age, done, foot, dog, take, taker, pass, cover, world, graduate, go, went, brush growth, privileged, handed, study)

46. home (work, sick, made, maker, body, coming, land, stead)

47. down (stairs, town, pour, hill, stream, fall, grade, right)

48. head (light, ache, band, first, quarters, phone, line, work, strong)

94   MISSING COMPOUND

Materials needed
¼ sheet of lined paper for each student
pencil for each student
dictionary

☒ total group activity
☐ individual activity
☐ partner activity

Total Group Activity

Give the students a few minutes to write several compound words. Stress that they must be true compound words, that is, two words forming a single word with no hyphens or spaces between the words. Encourage them to use a dictionary to settle questions.

Call on a student to read *half* of one of his or her compound words. The other students try to guess the word by adding another word either *before* or *after* the word that was named. For example:

side could become *outside* or *sidewalk*

The person who guesses the word becomes the leader for the next game and calls on volunteers to guess his or her mystery compound word. The identical compound word may not be used again, but half of a compound word may be used multiple times.

95   GUESS MY WORD

Materials needed
none

- ☒ total group activity
- ☐ individual activity
- ☐ partner activity

Total Group Activity

Tell the students that you have a list of words, each of which begins with a _____ (name the specific letter of the alphabet). Challenge them to discover the mystery words by listening to your clues. The following list provides ten clues each for the letters <u>W</u> , <u>Y</u> , <u>D</u> , <u>P</u> , <u>C</u> , and <u>S</u> .

Words that Begin with <u>W</u>

1. Something that makes the trees move.   **(wind)**
2. The season that follows fall.   **(winter)**
3. Something that you burn in a fireplace.   **(wood)**
4. The opposite of man.   **(woman)**
5. Another word for tepee.   **(wigwam)**
6. Something that is cut from sheep.   **(wool)**
7. The animal that tricked Little Red Riding Hood.   **(wolf)**
8. An insect that has a very painful sting.   **(wasp)**
9. The part of a candle that burns.   **(wick)**
10. A bird that pecks holes in trees.   **(woodpecker)**

Words that Begin with <u>Y</u>

1. The opposite of old.   **(young)**
2. The ground that surrounds a building.   **(yard)**
3. The day before today.   **(yesterday)**
4. A type of heavy thread that is used for knitting.   **(yarn)**
5. The color of butter.   **(yellow)**
6. What you sometimes do when you are tired.   **(yawn)**
7. Another name for 365 days.   **(year)**
8. The yellow part of an egg.   **(yolk)**
9. Something that is used to make bread rise.   **(yeast)**
10. People often do this at football games.   **(yell)**

Words that Begin with <u>D</u>

1. The last month of the year.   **(December)**
2. A person whose job it is to take care of people's teeth. **(dentist)**
3. Being unable to hear.   **(deaf)**
4. A weed that has bright yellow flowers.   **(dandelion)**
5. Where students keep their books and papers at school. **(desks)**

6. What you sometimes do at night while you are asleep.   (dream)

7. The name of a group of reptiles that lived a long, long time ago.   (dinosaurs)

8. The opposite of light.   (dark)

9. The meaning of a word.   (definition)

10. The time of day when the sun first starts to rise.   (dawn)

Words that Begin with P

1. A sea bird that looks like it is wearing a black coat.   (penguin)

2. A large piece of white cloth used when someone jumps from a plane.   (parachute)

3. A cute black and white animal that looks like a bear.   (panda)

4. A brightly colored bird that can be taught to say words.   (parrot)

5. A small lake.   (pond)

6. An animal that plays dead when it is frightened.   ('possum)

7. A bird with beautiful feathers that it can spread in a fan shape.   (peacock)

8. Someone who puts in pipes or repairs them.   (plumber)

9. To get ready for something.   (prepare)

10. A white, roundish jewel that comes from the inside of an oyster.   (pearl)

Words that Begin with C

1. You use it to tell time.   (clock)

2. You'll be happy when you're old enough to drive it.   (car)

3. You eat it off the cob.   (corn)

4. It is dark and bats live in it.   (cave)

5. You sometimes have it for your birthday.   (cake)

6. This holiday comes on the 25th of December.   (Christmas)

7. An animal that turns into a butterfly.   (caterpillar)

8. Your teacher works there when she teaches.   (classroom)

9. A special bed for a baby that rocks back and forth.   (cradle)

10. This is good to have if the electricity goes off.   (candle)

Words that Begin with S

1. You find these on a beach.   (shells)

2. This is used to dig.   (shovel)

3. It is cold, wet, and white.   (snow)

4. You use this when you wash your hands.   (soap)

5. The season when new plants start to grow.   (Spring)

6. A special ice cream treat.   (sundae)

7. A place to buy food.   (supermarket)

8. This used to be hitched to a horse so people could ride across the snow in it.   (sleigh)

9. If your arm is hurt it might be put in this.   (sling)

10. This is what all the bones in your body are called.   (skeleton)

96   BEGINNING, MIDDLE, OR END?

Materials needed
none

☒ total group activity
☐ individual activity
☐ partner activity

Total Group Activity

Name the letter of the alphabet and then read the following list of words for it. The designated letter will be somewhere within each word; at the beginning, middle, or end.

If students hear the letter at the *beginning* of the word, they should hold up their left fist. If they hear the letter at the *end* of the word, they should hold up their right fist. If they hear the letter in the *middle* of the word, they should hold up both fists while touching.

The following list provides twenty-four words each for the letters *D, L, P, F, C,* and *V.*

Variation

Materials needed
lined paper
pencils

Students fold a piece of paper into four columns. The first column is numbered 1 to 24; *B,* for beginning, is written at the top of the second column; *M,* for middle is written at the top of the third column; and *E,* for end, is written at the top of the fourth column.

Designate a letter from the following list and tell them they are to listen for this sound in each of the words. Then read the number and the word from the list. Students should indicate whether they heard the specified sound at the beginning, middle, or end of the word by placing a checkmark in the appropriate column to the right of the specified number.

D WORDS		L WORDS		P WORDS	
1. muddy	**(M)**	1. leaf	**(B)**	1. poem	**(B)**
2. dollar	**(B)**	2. wheel	**(E)**	2. soup	**(E)**
3. shade	**(E)**	3. lunch	**(B)**	3. sleeping	**(M)**
4. leader	**(M)**	4. silly	**(M)**	4. leap	**(E)**
5. loud	**(E)**	5. laugh	**(B)**	5. push	**(B)**
6. double	**(B)**	6. yelling	**(M)**	6. open	**(M)**
7. dark	**(B)**	7. pencil	**(E)**	7. pen	**(B)**
8. paddle	**(M)**	8. lost	**(B)**	8. step	**(E)**
9. sliding	**(M)**	9. nail	**(E)**	9. soapy	**(M)**
10. door	**(B)**	10. squeal	**(E)**	10. paddle	**(B)**
11. cried	**(E)**	11. lake	**(B)**	11. supper	**(M)**
12. ladder	**(M)**	12. roll	**(E)**	12. shape	**(E)**
13. dime	**(B)**	13. light	**(B)**	13. dropping	**(M)**

D WORDS

14. under	(M)
15. played	(E)
16. sad	(E)
17. ready	(M)
18. dirt	(B)
19. inside	(E)
20. dot	(B)
21. hiding	(M)
22. tried	(E)
23. head	(E)
24. down	(B)

L WORDS

14. balloon	(M)
15. smile	(E)
16. hello	(M)
17. feel	(E)
18. line	(B)
19. pool	(E)
20. leap	(B)
21. while	(E)
22. July	(M)
23. tell	(E)
24. listen	(B)

P WORDS

14. part	(B)
15. snap	(E)
16. skip	(E)
17. pillow	(B)
18. happy	(M)
19. pick	(B)
20. sleep	(E)
21. clap	(E)
22. pencil	(B)
23. sloppy	(M)
24. penny	(B)

F WORDS

1. roof	(E)
2. fast	(B)
3. muffin	(M)
4. stuff	(E)
5. fog	(B)
6. traffic	(M)
7. awful	(M)
8. safe	(E)
9. funny	(B)
10. refuse	(M)
11. fire	(B)
12. ruffle	(M)
13. leaf	(E)
14. filling	(B)
15. sofa	(M)
16. find	(B)
17. safe	(E)
18. filly	(B)
19. muffle	(M)
20. giraffe	(E)
21. fix	(B)
22. stiff	(E)
23. fumble	(B)
24. fight	(B)

C WORDS

1. attic	(E)
2. color	(B)
3. acorn	(M)
4. copy	(B)
5. balcony	(M)
6. candy	(B)
7. become	(M)
8. music	(E)
9. catch	(B)
10. cotton	(B)
11. second	(M)
12. magic	(E)
13. cabbage	(B)
14. jacket	(M)
15. cover	(B)
16. public	(E)
17. vacuum	(M)
18. camera	(B)
19. calendar	(B)
20. basic	(E)
21. because	(M)
22. castle	(B)
23. became	(M)
24. carpenter	(B)

V WORDS

1. brave	(E)
2. seven	(M)
3. voice	(B)
4. cover	(M)
5. carve	(E)
6. even	(M)
7. violet	(B)
8. five	(E)
9. view	(B)
10. flavor	(M)
11. vowels	(B)
12. wave	(E)
13. navy	(M)
14. vacation	(B)
15. woven	(M)
16. have	(E)
17. vase	(B)
18. leaving	(M)
19. save	(E)
20. village	(B)
21. never	(M)
22. live	(E)
23. vitamin	(B)
24. stove	(E)

97   DOUBLE-DUTY Y

Materials needed

Total Group Activity

Remind students that the letter *y* is both a vowel and a consonant. When it is a vowel it is usually pronounced like a long *e* as in *silly*, or as a long *i* as in *sky*. Occasionally it has a short *i* sound as in *bicycle*. At the beginning of a word, *y* is always a consonant.

Read the following list of words. If *y* is a consonant, the students should put their thumbs up. If it is a vowel, they should put their thumbs down.

Is Y a Consonant or a Vowel Here?

1. story	**(down)**	15. yank	**(up)**	28. youngster	**(up)**
2. yard	**(up)**	16. penny	**(down)**	29. dry	**(down)**
3. happy	**(down)**	17. any	**(down)**	30. yet	**(up)**
4. baby	**(down)**	18. young	**(up)**	31. yeast	**(up)**
5. year	**(up)**	19. bicycle	**(down)**	32. many	**(down)**
6. fly	**(down)**	20. you	**(up)**	33. your	**(up)**
7. yellow	**(up)**	21. yoke	**(up)**	34. country	**(down)**
8. yours	**(up)**	22. try	**(down)**	35. yo-yo	**(up)**
9. funny	**(down)**	23. try	**(down)**	36. early	**(down)**
10. yourself	**(up)**	24. empty	**(down)**	37. fry	**(down)**
11 lazy	**(down)**	25. yarn	**(up)**	38. yacht	**(up)**
12. sunny	**(down)**	26. very	**(down)**	39. hurry	**(down)**
13. yes	**(up)**	27. pretty	**(down)**	40. bakery	**(down)**
14. family	**(down)**				

98   LETTER SUBSTITUTION GAME

Materials needed
chalkboard
chalk
eraser

[X] total group activity
[ ] individual activity
[ ] partner activity

Total Group Activity

On the chalkboard write a word from the following list. Have the students mentally substitute a letter to form a new word following the game rules below. Call on a student to write the new word on the chalkboard. Then have this student choose the next person to go to the board.

Make clear which letter or letters may be changed. When using List 1 only the initial letter may be changed. When using List 2 *either* the first letter or the last letter may be changed, but in any one turn *both* letters may not be changed. For example, for the word *boot*:

book } Either of these words would be correct, because only one letter was changed in each new
loot } word.

soon   This word would not be correct, because both the initial and final letters were changed.

When using List 3 either the initial letter or the vowel may be changed. And for List 4 the initial letter, the vowel, or the final letter may be changed.

If the students are uncertain about their new word, let them whisper it to you as a check before writing it on the chalkboard. Younger students especially will need verification when working with words that sound similar, but are spelled differently (for example, *mom, palm*).

LIST 1   *(Change initial letter only):*

hat	pet	dot
night	cake	cold
bug	cap	jump
mad	hill	

LIST 2   *(Change initial or final letter): (Optional: Substitute blend, digraph, or single consonant for initial letter or change final letter)*

pin	pig	dog
mad	book	cup
tub	car	pool

LIST 3   *(Change initial letter or vowel):*

back	bang
sing	bell
ball	sick

LIST 4   *(Change initial letter, vowel, or final letter):*

rug	hot	jet
hen	bag	cap
mop	sun	hid
sad		

99   LAST TO FIRST

Materials needed
none

☒ total group activity
☐ individual activity
☐ partner activity

Total Group Activity

Have a student point to someone, say a word, and spell it. Within the count of five, the second student must say a new word that begins with the *last letter of the word* given by the first student, point to another student, and spell the new word to repeat the process. No words may be repeated, nor should the same student be called on within any round. If a word is repeated or a student cannot think of a word before the count of five, the leader calls on a different student. For example:

> school, s-c-h-o-o-l
> lunch, l-u-n-c-h
> horse, h-o-r-s-e
> elephant, e-l-e-p-h-a-n-t
> tooth, t-o-o-t-h
> (The next word could not be *horse*
> because it has already been used in this round.)

Initially you should set the pace for the count of five by slowly raising one finger at a time while softly saying the numbers. Once the pace is set, the leader can assume the job of counting.

For younger students, require that the words be at least four letters in length. Move to five-letter words as the students become sure of themselves. Older students can begin with five-letter words.

To relieve pressure in the beginning, instruct the leader to call on only those students who have their hands raised. Later have everyone stand and instruct students to sit after they've had a turn. When everyone is seated, have the entire class stand again and begin a new round.

100 CATEGORY SPELLING

Materials needed
¼ sheet of paper for each student
pencil for each student
clock *or* timer

[X] total group activity
[ ] individual activity
[ ] partner activity

Total Group Activity

Name a letter of the alphabet (for example, *k*) and give the students a specified amount of time (two minutes or so) to write a three-letter word, a four-letter word, a five-letter word, and so on, each starting with the designated letter. Explain that they should be able to give a definition or clue for each of the words they write. For example, "This unlocks a door" **(key)**, "You fly me on a windy day" **(kite)**.

Choose a student to give only one clue about his or her three-letter word and to call on classmates until the word is discovered. The person who correctly identifies and *spells* the word gives the next definition using a four-letter word. Continue in this manner, increasing the length of the word each time, until no one has a word for the designated number of letters. Then start a new round by naming a new letter. If students guess a word, but are unable to spell it, they may ask someone to spell it for them. This enables all students to participate.

101   HOW MANY WAYS—

Materials needed
None

☒ total group activity
☐ individual activity
☐ partner activity

Total Group Activity

This is a good activity to teach children descriptive words that go beyond overused words like "big, small, good, bad, little, and fast."

Ask the students to think of as many words as possible that describe how an item on the following list might look, feel, taste, sound, or move. If they have difficulty thinking of ideas, ask leading questions such as, "If a house is very old, how might you describe it?" "If the house were new?" "If the house were far out in the country with no other hosues around?" and so on.

As in any brainstorming activity, accept any answer the student can back with good logic. Some sample answers are provided here.

How Many Ways Can—

1. a house look

(**ugly, old, dirty, old-fashioned, new, messy, beautiful, well-kept, deserted, abandoned...**)

2. a person feel

(**grumpy, mad, puzzled, ignorant, sick, confused, curious, horrified, angry, frightened, smug...**)

3. grass feel

(**soft, buggy, prickly, itchy, tickly, wet, soggy, damp, smooth, scratchy, dry, moist, thick, cool...**)

4. a piece of material look (*without naming colors*)

(**discolored, faded, ripped, bright, plain, colorful, smooth, rough, furry, warm, thin, thick...**)

5. a road look

(**slippery, muddy, dusty, bumpy, rough, smooth, holey, windy, straight, wide, narrow, sloped...**)

6. candy feel

(**sticky, smooth, gooey, hard, bumpy, squishy, rough, slick, crunchy, brittle, soft...**)

7. a tree look

(**huge, tiny, crooked, gnarled, decayed, twisted, tall, dead, sickly, colorful, sappy...**)

8. a lake look

(**clear, dirty, clean, mossy, swampy, icy, muddy, huge, sandy, deep, shallow, crowded...**)

9. a rock feel

(**hard, smooth, bumpy, rough, jagged, wet, damp, hot, cold, sandy, gritty, sharp, mossy...**)

10. the tail of an animal look

(**furry, fuzzy, long, short, skinny, curved, curly, stumpy, pointed, fluffy, scaley, droopy...**)

11. smoke look (*without naming colors*)

(**thick, dangerous, swirly, still, scary, deadly, wispy, billowy...**)

12. an animal move

(**limp, trot, bound, race, glide, soar, flutter, scamper, gallop, slither...**)

13. a milkshake look (without naming colors or flavors)

(bubbly, thick, thin, lumpy, icy, runny, foamy, delicious, cooling, cold, yummy...)

14. a berry taste

(ripe, sweet, sour, bitter, rotten, awful, mushy, juicy, scrumptious...)

15. the seed of a plant look

(tiny, oval-shaped, large, enormous, prickly, smooth, round, spiked, feathery...)

16. a forest look

(inviting, threatening, cool, scary, refreshing, damp, colorful, smoky, frightening...)

17. a bell sound

(loud, low, tinkly, intermittent, shrill, dull, delicate, soft...)

18. the sky look

(dark, cloudy, stormy, colorful, foggy, clear, bright, threatening, overcast...)

19. the weather feel

(cool, warm, scorching, freezing, balmy, chilly, steaming, biting cold, damp...)

20. a piece of paper look (without naming colors)

Messy, neat, crumpled, blank, lined, unlined, colorful, festive, decorated, plain...)

21. a dog's hair feel

(smooth, silky, bristly, slick, sticky, wet, soft, fluffy, fuzzy, warm...)

22. a giant look

(huge, tall, ugly, mean, enormous, scary, cruel, menacing, friendly...)

23. a palace look

(gorgeous, decorated, glittering, enormous, imposing, awe-inspiring...)

24. a yell sound

(threatening, friendly, inviting, happy, joyous, excited, worried, scary...)

25. people show how they feel

(frown, smile, grin, yell, clap, giggle, cry, shake, pace, fidget...)

102   WHAT'S YOUR REACTION?

Materials needed
none

☒ total group activity
☐ individual activity
☐ partner activity

Total Group Activity

Have the students mentally picture one of the scenes from the following list. Encourage them to use words that convey exactly what they are thinking, feeling, or seeing, when answering these questions for each situation:

—Tell your reaction in one sentence.
—What descriptive words could you use to tell what you see, hear, touch, smell, or taste?

What's Your Reaction?

1. You are caught outside in a severe rain storm.
2. You go on your first roller coaster ride.
3. You and your family spend a day at the amusement park.
4. You take a walk in the woods on a fall day.
5. You're watching a large Fourth of July fireworks display.
6. You and your friend sneak into a very, very old deserted house.
7. You dive into a swimming pool on a hot summer day.
8. You go boating on a lake.
9. You go fishing with your dad.
10. You see a forest fire nearby.

103   SIMILES

Materials needed

Total Group Activity

Children always enjoy creating similes. In this activity encourage them to vary their similes from the standard ones. For example, if the students offer "white as snow" for the word *white,* ask, "What else is white? Think of things you could compare that perhaps no one else has ever thought of."

Using *white* as an example, clarify the difference between words that signify "whiteness" (clouds, snow, whipped cream) and things that may be white but could also be some other color (crayon, paint, table). Have them discuss the relative strengths and weaknesses of the following: "white as paint" and "white as a cotton ball"; "yellow as a crayon" and "yellow as a daffodil." Guide them to realize that a good simile stimulates a strong mental picture.

As in any creative thinking activity, accept any answer the student can back with good reasoning. Sample answers are provided here.

Create Similes for—

1. loud as

(a scream, a horn, a clap of thunder, an elephant trumpeting, a bass drum, a tiger roaring, a foghorn, a nuclear explosion, a broken muffler...)

2. rough as

(sandpaper, a rock, a shark's skin, the bark of a tree, sand, cement, gravel, a cat's tongue, old chipped paint, the comb of a chicken...)

3. pretty as

(leaves shining in the sun, a sunset, stars at night, flowers, a rainbow, a butterfly, rocks under water...)

4. quiet as

(a whisper, Santa Claus, a caterpillar, a germ, the Easter Bunny, a butterfly, a deer, a ghost, a worm, a breeze, a leaf falling, the moon, a rabbit, the Tooth Fairy...)

5. red as

(fire, a road on a map, lava, a tongue, lipstick, a strawberry, a tomato...)

6. scary as

(a monster, Dracula, a ghost, a bat, walking alone at night, a nightmare, a haunted house, a vampire...)

7. soft as

(a powder puff, a dog's fur, a caterpillar, a cotton ball, a bunny, silk, a pillow, velvet, a feather...)

8. shy as

(a squirrel, a deer, a blushing boy, a turtle, a child on the first day of school, a raccoon...)

9. shiny as

(metal, a mirror, silver, crystal, the sun, a new car, a diamond, gold, a star, glass, snow in the sun, a marble...)

10. tiny as

(an ant, a fly, a germ, a spider, a flea, a dot, an atom, an aphid, a grain of salt *or* sand, a seed, a crumb...)

11. smooth as

(wet skin, a glass, plastic, a waxed car, a table top, a seal's skin, wet hair...)

12. stinky as

(a skunk, a stink bug, an onion, a rotten egg, a sweaty sock, a fish, a sewer, sour milk...)

13. squeaky as

(a new tennis shoe, an unoiled wheel, a door, a fingernail scraping a chalkboard, a throat with laryngitis...)

14. white as

(a ghost, a polar bear, whipped cream, cotton, shaving cream, chalk, a cloud, a lamb, a tooth, an eyeball, plaster of Paris...)

15. tall as

(a basketball palyer, a skyscraper, Godzilla, a telephone pole, a giant, a giraffe, Mount Everest, a redwood tree, the Eiffel Tower...)

16. big as

(an elephant, a school, the world, a Japanese wrestler, a football player, a diesel truck, the universe, a stadium...)

17. swift as

(a cheetah, a jaguar, a jet, a shooting star, a lizard, a racing car, the space shuttle, the speed of light, a meteor...)

18. cool as

(shade, a breeze, a pool, the early morning air, the ocean, a cat's paw, a mountain stream, a cave, a basement floor...)

19. cold as

(an ice cube, ice cream, snow, a freezer, the North Pole, Antarctica, an iceberg, hail, frost, a skating rink, liquid nitrogen...)

20. hot as

(a sunburn, the desert, the sun, an oven, lava, the center of the earth, a burning ember...)

21. dark as

(space, Halloween night, a tunnel, a cave, a hole, a movie theater, black ink, a unlit room...)

22. dry as

(the desert, chapped lips, a dry throat, an overcooked steak, sand, beef jerky, a cracker...)

23. round as

(a circle, a pizza, a globe, a ball, a coin, a glass, a pie, the world, a marble, a wheel, the sun, a nostril...)

24. ugly as

(a toad, a witch, a tarantula, Frankenstein's monster, a tomato bug, a slug, a hippopotamus...)

25. strong as

(a football player, an elephant, a weight lifter, a nuclear blast, King Kong, a hurricane, a Japanese wrestler, an earthquake...)

104   NAME THE OPPOSITE

Materials needed
none

☒ total group activity
☐ individual activity
☐ partner activity

Total Group Activity

Name a word on the following list and ask the students to think of its antonym (opposite). Emphasize that in some cases there may be more than one correct answer. Ask them to raise a hand if they have an answer and to put it down as soon as someone else says the word they were thinking of. Call on anyone whose hand remains up. Besides providing needed practice with antonyms, this activity enables you to locate the students who are confused about antonyms and synonyms.

Accept any answer the student can back with good logic. Sample answers are provided here.

Name the Opposite for—

1. come	**(go)**	25. old	**(new)**	49. few	**(many)**
2. brother	**(sister)**	26. female	**(male)**	50. tame	**(wild)**
3. young	**(old)**	27. strong	**(weak)**	51. ceiling	**(floor)**
4. beginning	**(end)**	28. catch	**(throw)**	52. friend	**(enemy)**
5. dead	**(alive)**	29. in	**(out)**	53. land	**(water)**
6. up	**(down)**	30. hello	**(goodbye)**	54. smooth	**(rough)**
7. happy	**(sad)**	31. glad	**(sad)**	55. war	**(peace)**
8. easy	**(hard)**	32. uncle	**(aunt)**	56. top	**(bottom)**
9. noisy	**(quiet)**	33. soft	**(hard)**	57. same	**(different)**
10. clean	**(dirty)**	34. over	**(under)**	58. high	**(low)**
11. sit	**(stand)**	35. laugh	**(cry)**	59. find	**(lose)**
12. inside	**(outside)**	36. night	**(day)**	60. fat	**(thin)**
13. yes	**(no)**	37. wide	**(narrow)**	61. loose	**(tight)**
14. take	**(give)**	38. summer	**(winter)**	62. asleep	**(awake)**
15. back	**(front)**	39. deep	**(shallow)**	63. full	**(empty)**
16. beautiful	**(ugly)**	40. large	**(small)**	64. humility	**(pride)**
17. father	**(mother)**	41. add	**(subtract)**	65. play	**(work)**
18. smile	**(frown)**	42. start	**(stop)**	66. long	**(short)**
19. big	**(small)**	43. late	**(early)**	67. fair	**(unfair)**
20. woman	**(man)**	44. short	**(tall)**	68. hot	**(cold)**
21. found	**(lost)**	45. buy	**(sell)**	69. rich	**(poor)**
22. sick	**(well)**	46. Mr.	**(Mrs.)**	70. good	**(bad)**
23. boy	**(girl)**	47. lie	**(admit)**	71. difficult	**(easy)**
24. white	**(black)**	48. wise	**(foolish)**	72. sweet	**(sour)**

73. true	(false)	98. stretch	(shrink)	123. lend	(borrow)
74. on	(off)	99. north	(south)	124. permanent	(temporary)
75. thaw	(freeze)	100. before	(after)	125. future	(past)
76. cautious	(reckless)	101. idle	(busy)	126. polite	(rude)
77. life	(death)	102. love	(hate)	127. nothing	(all)
78. behind	(ahead)	103. east	(west)	128. visible	(invisible)
79. open	(close, shut)	104. sharp	(dull)	129. entrance	(exit)
80. dark	(light)	105. push	(pull)	130. escape	(capture)
81. forget	(remember)	106. thick	(thin)	131. familiar	(strange)
82. fast	(slow)	107. start	(finish)	132. reward	(punish)
83. gentle	(rough)	108. near	(far)	133. seldom	(often)
84. careful	(careless)	109. yours	(mine)	134. awkward	(graceful)
85. sink	(float)	110. above	(below)	135. sorrow	(joy)
86. all	(none)	111. straight	(crooked)	136. eager	(reluctant)
87. left	(right)	112. follow	(lead)	137. doubt	(believe)
88. better	(worse)	113. expensive	(cheap)	138. ancient	(modern)
89. win	(lose)	114. question	(answer)	139. fiction	(nonfiction)
90. lower	(raise, upper)	115. honest	(dishonest)	140. accept	(refuse)
91. big	(little)	116. here	(there)	141. forbid	(allow)
92. guess	(know)	117. forward	(backward)	142. tense	(relaxed)
93. huge	(tiny)	118. against	(for)	143. approve	(disapprove)
94. part	(whole)	119. proud	(ashamed)	144. incredible	(believable)
95. present	(absent)	120. increase	(decrease)	145. abundant	(scarce)
96. arrive	(depart)	121. guilty	(innocent)	146. genuine	(fake)
97. first	(last)	122. success	(failure)	147. help	(hinder)

105   WHAT'S THE MISSING WORD?

Materials needed

Total Group Activity

Read the following sentences and have the students suggest possible "missing words" that start with the letter you designate. Students should try to supply colorful words as often as possible. Sample responses are provided here, but all logical answers should be accepted.

What's the Missing Word?

1. When Johnny heard the good news he _____ home.
   - (A) The word begins with r.   **(raced, ran, rushed)**
   - (B) The word begins with h.   **(hurried, hustled)**
   - (C) The word begins with d.   **(dashed)**
   - (D) The word begins with f.   **(flew)**

2. We rode our bikes along the _____.
   - (A) The word begins with s.   **(street, sidewalk)**
   - (B) The word begins with p.   **(path)**
   - (C) The word begins with t.   **(trail)**
   - (D) The word begins with r.   **(road, roadway)**

3. It was a _____ storm.
   - (A) The word begins with t.   **(terrible)**
   - (B) The word begins with h.   **(horrible)**
   - (C) The word begins with a.   **(awful)**
   - (D) The word begins with d.   **(dreadful)**
   - (E) The word begins with s.   **(severe)**

4. When Freddy told his story we all _____.
   - (A) The word begins with l.   **(laughed)**
   - (B) The word begins with s.   **(smiled)**
   - (C) The word begins with c.   **(chuckled)**
   - (D) The word begins with g.   **(grinned, giggled)**

5. Mother said, "What in the world have you been doing? Just look at your _____ clothing!"

   (A) The word begins with <u>s</u>.   (soiled, stained, spotted)

   (B) The word begins with <u>d</u>.   (dirty)

   (C) The word begins with <u>f</u>.   (filthy)

   (D) The word begins with <u>g</u>.   (grimy)

6. We had a _____ time on vacation.

   (A) The word begins with <u>w</u>.   (wonderful)

   (B) The word begins with <u>s</u>.   (splendid, superb)

   (C) The word begins with <u>m</u>.   (marvelous)

   (D) The word begins with <u>f</u>.   (fabulous)

   (E) The word begins with <u>e</u>.   (enjoyable)

7. The homes were badly damaged by the _____.

   (A) The word begins with <u>s</u>.   (storm)

   (B) The word begins with <u>h</u>.   (hurricane)

   (C) The word begins with <u>t</u>.   (tornado)

   (D) The word begins with <u>b</u>.   (blizzard)

8. The stars were _____ in the sky.

   (A) The word begins with <u>s</u>.   (sparkling, shining)

   (B) The word begins with <u>g</u>.   (glittering, gleaming, glowing)

   (D) The word begins with <u>t</u>.   (twinkling)

9. In the fairy tale, he was _____ of all the land.

   (A) The word begins with <u>k</u>.   (king)

   (B) The word begins with <u>r</u>.   (ruler)

   (C) The word begins with <u>e</u>.   (emperor)

   (D) The word begins with <u>m</u>.   (master)

10. My dog walks in a _____ way.

   (A) The word begins with <u>s</u>.   (strange)

   (B) The word begins with <u>u</u>.   (unusual)

   (C) The word begins with <u>o</u>.   (odd)

   (D) The word begins with <u>p</u>.   (peculiar)

11. When I awakened Dad, he was very _____.

   (A) The word begins with <u>c</u>.   (cross, cranky)

   (B) The word begins with <u>g</u>.   (grouchy)

   (C) The word begins with <u>i</u>.   (irritated, irritable)

   (D) The word begins with <u>a</u>.   (annoyed)

12. The soldiers ——— back to their
    campsite.

    (A) The word begins with <u>m</u>.   **(marched)**

    (B) The word begins with <u>t</u>.   **(trudged)**

    (C) The word begins with <u>s</u>.   **(staggered)**

    (D) The word begins with <u>h</u>.   **(hiked, hobbled)**

13. The ——— puppy tugged at the
    sleeve of my coat.

    (A) The word begins with <u>p</u>.   **(playful)**

    (B) The word begins with <u>m</u>.   **(mischievous)**

    (C) The word begins with <u>f</u>.   **(frisky)**

    (D) The word begins with <u>i</u>.   **(impish)**

14. The book was so ——— that I
    couldn't put it down.

    (A) The word begins with <u>f</u>.   **(fascinating, funny)**

    (B) The word begins with <u>i</u>.   **(interesting, intriguing)**

    (C) The word begins with <u>e</u>.   **(exciting, entertaining)**

    (D) The word begins with <u>a</u>.   **(amusing, absorbing)**

15. When Judy walked outside she said,
    "What a ——— day."

    (A) The word starts with <u>c</u>.   **(cold, chilly)**

    (B) The word starts with <u>b</u>.   **(beautiful)**

    (C) The word begins with <u>l</u>.   **(lovely)**

    (D) The word begins with <u>d</u>.   **(dreary, dreadful)**

16. Your grandmother is such a ———
    person.

    (A) The word starts with <u>f</u>.   **(friendly)**

    (B) The word starts with <u>i</u>.   **(thoughtful)**

    (C) The word begins with <u>c</u>.   **(considerate)**

    (D) The word begins with <u>p</u>.   **(pleasant)**

106   SYNONYM/ANTONYM

Materials needed
none

☒ total group activity
☐ individual activity
☐ partner activity

Total Group Activity

Read a pair of words from the list below and have the students identify whether they are synonyms or antonyms. If the words are synonyms (mean the same thing or nearly the same thing), they should clasp their hands together. If the words are antonyms (opposites), they should point their thumbs outward.

Pause after reading each pair of words. Students signal their response when you say, "Now."

Are They Synonyms or Antonyms?

1. start/begin	**(synonyms)**	26. friend/enemy	**(antonyms)**
2. beautiful/ugly	**(antonyms)**	27. awful/terrible	**(synonyms)**
3. awake/asleep	**(antonyms)**	28. late/early	**(antonyms)**
4. afraid/scared	**(synonyms)**	29. sick/ill	**(synonyms)**
5. fast/quick	**(synonyms)**	30. question/answer	**(antonyms)**
6. start/finish	**(antonyms)**	31. sparkling/glittering	**(synonyms)**
7. jump/leap	**(synonyms)**	32. smooth/rough	**(antonyms)**
8. near/close	**(synonyms)**	33. tame/wild	**(antonyms)**
9. find/lose	**(antonyms)**	34. let/allow	**(synonyms)**
10. cool/warm	**(antonyms)**	35. wreck/destroy	**(synonyms)**
11. noisy/loud	**(synonyms)**	36. clean/soiled	**(antonyms)**
12. ask/answer	**(antonyms)**	37. give/receive	**(antonyms)**
13. giggle/laugh	**(synonyms)**	38. help/assist	**(synonyms)**
14. same/different	**(antonyms)**	39. damage/fix	**(antonyms)**
15. middle/center	**(synonyms)**	40. shy/timid	**(synonyms)**
16. full/empty	**(antonyms)**	41. never/always	**(antonyms)**
17. enormous/gigantic	**(synonyms)**	42. finish/complete	**(synonyms)**
18. enter/leave	**(antonyms)**	43. try/attempt	**(synonyms)**
19. war/peace	**(antonyms)**	44. accept/reject	**(antonyms)**
20. dangerous/unsafe	**(synonyms)**	45. depart/leave	**(synonyms)**
21. find/discover	**(synonyms)**	46. glad/delighted	**(synonyms)**
22. speak/talk	**(synonyms)**	47. reckless/careful	**(antonyms)**
23. remember/forget	**(antonyms)**	48. tired/weary	**(synonyms)**
24. bright/dull	**(antonyms)**	49. construct/destroy	**(antonyms)**
25. mad/angry	**(synonyms)**	50. scare/frighten	**(synonyms)**

107   PUZZLING PLURALS

Materials needed
none

☒ total group activity
☐ individual activity
☐ partner activity

Total Group Activity

Read the following words and have the students give the plural form of each.

coat	**(coats)**
calf	**(calves)**
box	**(boxes)**
goose	**(geese)**
sheep	**(sheep)**

Point out that plurals have a variety of sounds, for example, *s*, *es*, and *ves*. In addition, in irregular plurals such as *geese*, the word changes completely, whereas in other words such as *sheep*, the plural and singular forms are identical.

Read the following groups of three words, calling on volunteers to repeat the words in the same order but in their plural forms. For example, if you said, "tooth, cat, mouse," they would reply, "teeth, cats, mice." (With younger students, simplify the task by reading only one or two words and then asking for the plural form.)

Students enjoy this activity since it requires remembering and quick thinking. By keeping it moving at a fast pace, you'll find them suddenly getting caught saying "foots, mouses, etc.," which results in a good laugh for all. Nonetheless, the activity provides an excellent opportunity to reinforce the *sound* of correct plural forms. This concept can be extended at a later time and applied to written work.

What Are the Plurals of—

1. wish, child, boy   **(wishes, children, boys)**
2. monkey, sheep, wolf   **(monkeys, sheep, wolves)**
3. goose, toy, bush   **(geese, toys, bushes)**
4. life, day, moose   **(lives, days, moose)**
5. turkey, man, hoof   **(turkeys, men, hooves)**
6. dish, fish, key   **(dishes, fish, keys)**
7. elf, foot, country   **(elves, feet, countries)**
8. lunch, lady, deer   **(lunches, ladies, deer)**
9. branch, mouse, balloon   **(branches, mice, balloons)**
10. trout, robot, inch   **(trout, robots, inches)**
11. tooth, ladder, leaf   **(teeth, ladders, leaves)**
12. spider, ox, witch   **(spiders, oxen, witches)**
13. woman, tiger, bunch   **(women, tigers, bunches)**
14. scarf, grandchild, airplane   **(scarves, grandchildren, airplanes)**
15. goose, cloud, wife   **(geese, clouds, wives)**
16. room, sheep, switch   **(rooms, sheep, switches)**
17. actress, foot, snail   **(actresses, feet, snails)**
18. moose, light, box   **(moose, lights, boxes)**
19. book, tooth, loaf   **(books, teeth, loaves)**
20. fox, deer, star   **(foxes, deer, stars)**
21. recess, hotel, woman   **(recesses, hotels, women)**
22. ox, ship, calf   **(oxen, ships, calves)**
23. child, bicycle, tax   **(children, bicycles, taxes)**
24. business, rose, man   **(businesses, roses, men)**
25. ax, mouse, noise   **(axes, mice, noises)**
26. voice, goose, knife   **(voices, geese, knives)**
27. horse, foot, nose   **(horses, feet, noses)**
28. glass, mouse, eye   **(glasses, mice, eyes)**
29. race, tooth, shelf   **(races, teeth, shelves)**
30. woman, pass, vote   **(women, passes, votes)**

108   HAM AND EGGS: WORDS THAT GO TOGETHER

Materials needed
none

☒ total group activity
☐ individual activity
☐ partner activity

Total Group Activity

This is a game of word pairs, or words that go together. Give the first word of a pair from the following list and ask the students to think of a word to complete it. For instance, if you said "ham and _____," they might say "eggs." Students raise their hands as soon as they identify the missing word, or you can give a hand signal and have the students respond in unison.

While sample answers are provided here, any answer that can be backed with logical reasoning should be accepted.

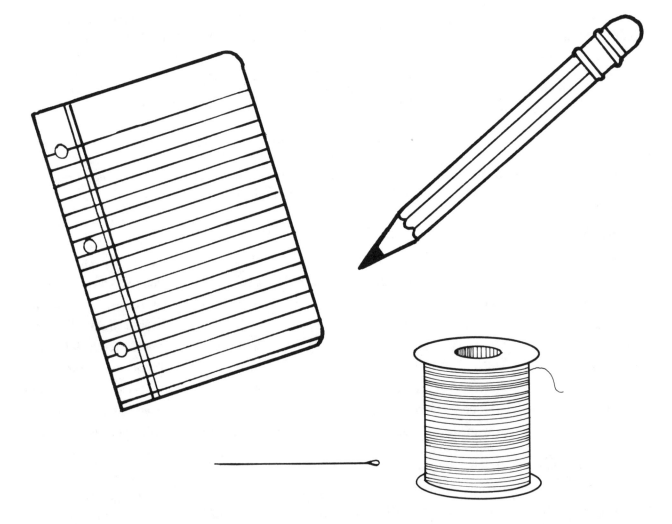

Variation: Divide the class into two teams and have each team count off. Say the first part of a word pair. Players on each team compete in numerical order to be the first to say the word that completes the pair. The first correct answer wins a point for that player's team.

The game ends when all players have had one turn. The team with the most points wins.

Pair These Words

1. boys and (**girls**)
2. pots and (**pans**)
3. bread and (**butter**)
4. salt and (**pepper**)
5. bacon and (**eggs**)
6. cake and (**ice cream**)
7. shoes and (**socks**)
8. grandmother and (**grandfather**)
9. soap and (**water**)
10. stop and (**go**)
11. king and (**queen**)
12. up and (**down**)
13. brother and (**sister**)
14. cat and (**dog, mouse**)
15. hot and (**cold**)
16. pencil and (**paper**)
17. night and (**day**)
18. over and (**under, out**)
19. cup and (**saucer**)
20. left and (**right**)
21. in and (**out**)
22. thunder and (**lightning**)
23. husband and (**wife**)
24. high and (**low**)
25. nickel and (**dime**)
26. needle and (**thread, pins**)
27. bat and (**ball**)
28. cap and (**gown**)
29. comb and (**brush**)
30. men and (**women**)
31. meat and (**potatoes**)
32. raincoat and (**umbrella**)
33. uncle and (**aunt**)
34. coffee and (**cream**)
35. lock and (**key**)
36. war and (**peace**)
37. crackers and (**cheese**)
38. north and (**south**)
39. hit and (**run**)
40. snow and (**ice**)
41. corned beef and (**cabbage**)
42. east and (**west**)
43. stars and (**stripes**)
44. army and (**navy**)
45. strawberries and (**cream**)
46. shirt and (**tie**)
47. sugar and (**spice**)
48. sickness and (**health**)
49. thick and (**thin**)
50. touch and (**go**)

109   CEMENT MIXER GAME

Materials needed
none

☒ total group activity
☐ individual activity
☐ partner activity

Total Group Activity

One child is chosen to leave the room. The remainder of the class selects a word (Example: *hop*). Each student thinks of a sentence using this word. However, instead of saying the secret word, they should substitute the words "cement mixer." (Example: "Can you *cement mixer* up and down on one foot?"

When the child returns to the room, he or she calls on students to say their sentences until the mystery word is discovered. The student whose sentence "unlocked" the word leaves the room and the game continues as above.

Variation: Sometimes have the students use verbs and other times specify that they must use nouns.

110   HOMONYM TAG

Materials needed
chalkboard
chalk
eraser

☒ total group activity
☐ individual activity
☐ partner activity

Total Group Activity

On the chalkboard write approximately fifteen pairs of homonyms from the following list. Have everyone stand, then call on a student to choose a homonym and slowly spell it. Then call on another student. The second student repeats the word and its spelling, then uses it in a sentence. The person who chose the homonym indicates whether the word was used correctly. If the second student was right, he or she names the next homonym. Otherwise the first person continues calling on classmates until a correct response is given. Students should sit down after they have had a turn.

When a homonym is used, place a check mark beside the *pair of words*. When a pair has three check marks, erase both words.

Variation: The player who is the caller uses one of the words in a sentence. The student called on must (1) identify and spell the word or (2) use the "partner" word in a sentence.

Homonyms

1. to, too, two
2. wood, would
3. no, know
4. they're, there, their
5. dear, deer
6. week, weak
7. threw, through
8. by, buy, bye
9. hole, whole
10. road, rode
11. right, write, rite
12. piece, peace
13. one, won
14. for, four, fore
15. hour, our
16. past, passed
17. knows, nose
18. cent, sent, scent
19. some, sum

20. break, brake
21. flour, flower
22. meat, meet, mete
23. horse, hoarse
24. knead, need
25. hay, hey
26. find, fined
27. guessed, guest
28. role, roll
29. red, read
30. sail, sale
31. sew, so, sow
32. stair, stare
33. pedal, peddle
34. steak, stake
35. plain, plane
36. tale, tail
37. toe, tow
38. wade, weighed

39. waste, waist
40. capital, capitol
41. cell, sell
42. bored, board
43. heard, herd
44. cheap, cheep
45. knight, night
46. pause, paws
47. hair, hare
48. not, knot
49. creak, creek
50. heel, heal, he'll
51. die, dye
52. new, knew, gnu
53. chute, shoot
54. ceiling, sealing
55. peek, peak, pique
56. wring, ring
57. pail, pale

58. scene, seen
59. pair, pear, pare
60. sighed, side
61. principal, principle
62. pain, pane
63. sees, seas, seize
64. sword, soared
65. lesson, lessen
66. patients, patience
67. mist, missed
68. packed, pact
69. rain, reign, rein
70. billed, build
71. presents, presence
72. raise, rays, raze
73. straight, strait
74. sight, site, cite
75. compliment, complement

111   PREFIX JUMBLE

Materials needed
chalkboard
chalk
eraser

[X] total group activity
[ ] individual activity
[ ] partner activity

Total Group Activity

Students are often uncertain about prefixes. For example, is the word *inconsistent* or *unconsistent*? In this activity students experiment with a variety of words and prefixes and practice using correct forms.

Write the following prefixes on the chalkboard:

dis   un   in   im

Read one of the root words from the list below and ask for a definition. Call on a volunteer to make a new word by combining the root word with one of the prefixes on the chalkboard. Some of the words may take more than one prefix for different meanings. Ask another student to define the new word and explain the effect the prefix has on the root word. As a final step, ask a volunteer to use the new word in a sentence.

Add a Prefix to—

1. like	**(dislike; unlike)**	26. appropriate	**(inappropriate)**
2. correct	**(incorrect)**	27. trust	**(distrust)**
3. fair	**(unfair)**	28. mature	**(immature)**
4. polite	**(impolite)**	29. paid	**(unpaid)**
5. agree	**(disagree)**	30. adequate	**(inadequate)**
6. mobile	**(immobile)**	31. movable	**(immovable)**
7. accurate	**(inaccurate)**	32. connect	**(disconnect)**
8. believe	**(disbelieve)**	33. capable	**(incapable)**
9. perfect	**(imperfect)**	34. friendly	**(unfriendly)**
10. safe	**(unsafe)**	35. approve	**(disapprove)**
11. convenient	**(inconvenient)**	36. pure	**(impure)**
12. certain	**(uncertain)**	37. even	**(uneven)**
13. continue	**(discontinue)**	38. escapable	**(inescapable)**
14. possible	**(impossible)**	39. advantage	**(disadvantage)**
15. visible	**(invisible)**	40. mortal	**(immortal)**
16. able	**(unable; disable)**	41. clear	**(unclear)**
17. obey	**(disobey)**	42. consistent	**(inconsistent)**
18. practical	**(impractical)**	43. perceptible	**(imperceptible)**
19. curable	**(incurable)**	44. interested	**(disinterested)**
20. honest	**(dishonest)**	45. sane	**(insane)**
21. cut	**(uncut)**	46. wise	**(unwise)**
22. describable	**(indescribable)**	47. conspicuous	**(inconspicuous)**
23. patient	**(impatient)**	48. sure	**(unsure)**
24. appear	**(disappear)**	49. justice	**(injustice)**
25. harmed	**(unharmed)**		

112 SUFFIX PUZZLE

Materials needed
chalkboard
chalk
eraser

☒ total group activity
☐ individual activity
☐ partner activity

Total Group Activity

On the chalkboard write:

able   en   ful   ment

Read one of the root words from the following list. Call on a student to make a new word by combining the root word with one of the suffixes on the chalkboard. When the student has answered correctly, have him or her use the word in a sentence. Then call on a volunteer to give the definition of the new word and explain the effect the suffix has on the root word. Note that some root words may take more than one suffix for different meanings.

Add a Suffix to—

1. depend	**(dependable)**	23. like	**(likeable)**
2. tight	**(tighten)**	24. treat	**(treatment; treatable)**
3. care	**(careful)**	25. straight	**(straighten)**
4. enjoy	**(enjoyable; enjoyment)**	26. rest	**(restful)**
5. agree	**(agreement; agreeable)**	27. favor	**(favorable)**
6. beat	**(beaten)**	28. length	**(lengthen)**
7. thought	**(thoughtful)**	29. thank	**(thankful)**
8. comfort	**(comfortable)**	30. ship	**(shipment)**
9. help	**(helpful)**	31. move	**(movable; movement)**
10. amuse	**(amusement)**	32. eat	**(eaten; eatable)**
11. short	**(shorten)**	33. settle	**(settlement)**
12. appoint	**(appointment)**	34. trust	**(trustful)**
13. cheer	**(cheerful)**	35. invest	**(investment)**
14. argue	**(argument; arguable)**	36. desire	**(desirable)**
15. change	**(changeable)**	37. soft	**(soften)**
16. wood	**(wooden)**	38. govern	**(government; governable)**
17. assign	**(assignment; assignable)**	39. hope	**(hopeful)**
18. harm	**(harmful)**	40. pave	**(pavement)**
19. excite	**(excitement, excitable)**	41. deep	**(deepen)**
20. peace	**(peaceful; peaceable)**	42. fresh	**(freshen)**
21. bright	**(brighten)**	43. fright	**(frighten; frightful)**
22. use	**(useful; usable)**	44. pain	**(painful)**

113   WORD DERIVATIVE DETECTIVE

Materials needed
chalkboard
chalk
eraser

☒ total group activity
☐ individual activity
☐ partner activity

Total Group Activity

Explain that the English language derives from Greek and Latin. Therefore, knowledge of the more common word stems is extremely helpful in determining the meaning of unfamiliar words. This activity acquaints students with some of these stems and provides practice in using them.

Following are seven sets of questions to be read to the class. Each set helps the students discover and use one particular word stem.

Word Derivatives

1. A <u>tele</u>scope is used to see objects that are far away. (Write <u>tele</u> on the chalkboard.)

   A <u>tele</u>phone is used to transmit voices from a distance.

   What do you think <u>tele</u> means? (**to transmit from far away or a distance**)

   What do these words mean?

   A. a television (**the transmission of visual images and sound from a distance**)

   B. telethon (**a long television program, transmitted from a distance, often used to raise money for charity**)

   C. telegram (**a message sent by an electrical device—telegraph**)

2. <u>Micro</u>film is film on which documents are photographed in miniature. (Write <u>micro</u> on the chalkboard.)

   A <u>micro</u>phone is a device that makes small sounds louder.

   What do you think <u>micro</u> means? (**small**)

   What do these words mean?

   A. microscope (**an instrument that allows very small objects to be seen**)

   B. microbe (**a very small organism or germ**)

3. A <u>ped</u>al is a lever that is operated by the foot. (Write <u>ped</u> on the chalkboard.)

   A <u>ped</u>icure is the care of feet and toenails.

   What do you think <u>ped</u> means? (**foot**)

   What do these words mean?

   A. pedestrian (**a person who travels on foot**)

   B. biped (**an animal with two feet**)

   C. peddler (**a person who travels about on foot, selling goods**)

   D. pedestal (**an architectural support that has a base or foot**)

4. An <u>automat</u> is a restaurant where customers get food for themselves from vending machines.

   <u>Autonomy</u> means self-government.

   What do you think <u>auto</u> means? **(self)**

   What do these words mean?

   A. automobile **(a vehicle that is self-propelled)**

   B. automatic **(self-moving)**

   C. autobiography **(a story of a person's life written by that person)**

   D. autograph **(a person's signature)**

5. <u>Psychology</u> means the science or study of behavior and thinking processes. (Write <u>ology</u> and <u>logy</u> on the chalkboard.)

   <u>Bacteriology</u> is the scientific study of bacteria.

   What do you think <u>ology</u> or <u>logy</u> mean? **(study of, science of)**

   What do these words mean?

   A. zoology **(the science that deals with animals)**

   B. biology **(the science that deals with living organisms)**

   C. microbiology **(the science that deals with very small living organisms)**

   D. archaeology **(the study of people who lived in ancient times and their way of life)**

6. <u>Export</u> means to send or carry goods abroad. (Write <u>port</u> on the chalkboard.)

   A <u>porter</u> is someone who is hired to carry passengers' luggage.

   What do you think <u>port</u> means? **(carry)**

   What do these words mean?

   A. portable **(something that can be carried)**

   B. import **(to bring or carry goods from an outside source)**

   C. transportation **(the act of carrying goods or passengers from one place to another)**

   D. portage **(to carry boats and supplies over land)**

7. To <u>inscribe</u> means to write on paper, wood, or some other surface. (Write <u>scrib</u> and <u>script</u> on the chalkboard.)

   To <u>scribble</u> means to write hurriedly.

   What do you think <u>scrib</u> or <u>script</u> mean? **(write)**

   What do these words mean?

   A. prescription **(written instruction)**

   B. postscript **(a message written at the end of the letter; the abbreviation is P.S. and is used to denote an afterthought)**

   C. describe **(to convey or give an impression in words)**

114   THE FIVE W's

Materials needed
none

☒   total group activity
☐   individual activity
☐   partner activity

Total Group Activity

Explain the "five W's"—*who, what, when, where, why*—to the class. Then read one of the sentences from the five following lists and ask the students to identify the word or words that tell either who, what, when, where, or why in that sentence. Call on a volunteer to give the answer. Then ask for a show of hands to indicate how many agree. This keeps the entire class actively involved and allows you to quickly determine which students are having difficulty with the concept.

Variation: To make the activity more challenging, do not tell the students which word category you are using.

Variation (Grades 3–4)

Materials needed
chalkboard
chalk
eraser
Optional: clock *or* timer

Divide the class into two teams and number the players. Alternate giving questions to the teams, keeping score on the chalkboard.

Read a sentence and have the player identify the word or words that tell either who, what, when, where, or why.

Scoring should be handled in the following manner.

1. Team A's answer is correct—Team A earns one point. Play goes to the next player on Team B.

2. Team A's player makes a mistake and the next person on Team B spots the mistake and gives the correct answer—Team B gets the point and continues play.

3. Team A's player makes a mistake and the next player on Team B does not spot the mistake—no points are earned and Team B continues play.

The game ends when all students have had a turn or at the end of a designated time period. The team with the most points wins.

Which Word(s) Tell Who?

1. The newspaper had pictures of the astronauts floating in space. (**the astronauts**)
2. Our principal made an important announcement today. (**our principal**)
3. It was so sad when Charlotte died at the end of the book. (**Charlotte**)
4. During their act, the high wire artists did some unbelievable stunts. (**the high wire artists**)
5. My teacher assigned a lot of homework for tonight. (**my teacher**)
6. His grandfather is visiting from Florida. (**his grandfather**)
7. This Friday an author of children's books is going to come to our school. (**an author of children's books**)
8. The new school librarian told me about this book. (**the new school librarian**)
9. The broken glass was swept up by the school custodian. (**the school custodian**)
10. Last year my best friend was in a different classroom. (**my best friend**)

Which Word(s) Tell What?

1. During the storm a tree fell on our roof (**a tree**)
2. John hit the ball over the fence during our game yesterday. (**the ball**)
3. Today I finally learned how to draw a pentagon. (**a pentagon**)
4. Yesterday I polished my old bicycle. (**my old bicycle**)
5. Penny and Lori left their sweaters at the park. (**their sweaters**)
6. I heard a fantastic record last night. (**a fantastic record**)
7. During the storm the river near our house was overflowing. (**the river**)
8. Did you see the little curly-haired puppy at the pet shop? (**the little curly-haired puppy**)
9. Larry said he is going to wear his warmest coat today. (**his warmest coat**))
10. I saw a spectacular rainbow on my way to school this morning. (**a spectacular rainbow**)

Which Word(s) Tell When?

1. We had fun in school today. (**today**)
2. Nancy was late coming to school this morning. (**this morning**)
3. The sun rose early. (**early**)
4. The best time to look for sea life is at low tide. (**at low tide**)
5. Early in the morning I like to listen to the birds sing. (**early in the morning**)
6. On my birthday last year I got to go to the circus. (**last year**)
7. I always go fishing in the springtime. (**in the springtime**)
8. Jimmy made everyone laugh at lunchtime. (**at lunchtime**)
9. Let's play a game of basketball after school. (**after school**)
10. The day after tomorrow is my birthday. (**the day after tomorrow**)

Which Word(s) Tell Where?

1. When it began to thunder my dog ran into his doghouse. **(into his doghouse)**
2. We like to climb in our tree fort. **(in our tree fort)**
3. We played on the beach all day yesterday. **(on the beach)**
4. My cat likes to hide under the furniture. **(under the furniture)**
5. We planted our seeds one-quarter inch beneath the soil. **(one-quarter inch beneath the soil)**
6. I ran down the hill as fast as I could. **(down the hill)**
7. I got to stand near the sidelines during the football game. **(near the sidelines)**
8. I think you left your shoes under the bed. **(under the bed)**
9. The little boy peered behind the table. **(behind the table)**
10. Jack was so excited he threw the football up in the air. **(up in the air)**

Which Word(s) Tell Why?

1. Mother said she would drive us to school because we're running late. **(because we're running late)**
2. My mother took me to the doctor because I had a high temperature. **(because I had a high temperature)**
3. Since we finished early we got to choose what we wanted to do. **(since we finished early)**
4. School was closed for the day because of the storm. **(because of the storm)**
5. A lot of crops died because it didn't rain for a long time. **(because it didn't rain for a long time)**
6. Mother let me sleep late because I didn't get to bed until midnight. **(because I didn't get to bed until midnight)**
7. Since we sold the most tickets we got a special treat. **(since we sold the most tickets)**
8. I couldn't watch T.V. last night because I had so much homework. **(because I had so much homework)**
9. My friend is going to stay with us because her mom is in the hospital. **(because her mom is in the hospital)**
10. I got to invite a lot of friends over to my house because it was my birthday. **(because it was my birthday)**

115   PAST-TENSE PUZZLERS

Materials needed
none

☒ total group activity
☐ individual activity
☐ partner activity

Total Group Activity

This activity reinforces the *sound* of words in their past tense forms and also serves as a quick diagnostic tool.

Read the following words and ask the students to name the past tense form of each:

move	**(moved)**
push	**pushed**
bring	**(brought)**

Point out that *ed* is added to most words for events that have already taken place. However, not all past tenses are formed this way; some change their form. (For example: drive/drove, get/got.)

Read a group of three words from the following list. Call on a volunteer to repeat the words in the same order but in the past tense. For example, "walk, fly, freeze," becomes "walked, flew, froze." Go through this activity quickly to keep the interest level high.

Variation: With younger students, read the words one at a time and ask for the past tense after each word.

Give the Past Tenses for—

1.	see, talk, run	**(saw, talked, ran)**
2.	call, eat, sit	**(called, ate, sat)**
3.	give, write, laugh	**(gave, wrote, laughed)**
4.	wish, grow, speak	**(wished, grew, spoke)**
5.	know, freeze, miss	**(knew, froze, missed)**
6.	throw, rain, choose	**(threw, rained, chose)**
7.	move, sing, steal	**(moved, sang, stole)**
8.	ring, pick, break	**(rang, picked, broke)**
9.	bring, teach, explain	**(brought, taught, explained)**
10.	think, ride, come	**(thought, rode, came)**
11.	say, push, drink	**(said, pushed, drank)**
12.	lie, raise, use	**(lay, raised, used)**
13.	like, tear, draw	**(liked, tore, drew)**
14.	wear, save, blow	**(wore, saved, blew)**
15.	fly, leave, walk	**(flew, left, walked)**
16.	sit, give, look	**(sat, gave, looked)**
17.	do, stumble, take	**(did, stumbled, took)**
18.	play, fall, drive	**(played, fell, drove)**
19.	hide, color, feel	**(hid, colored, felt)**

20. draw, take, show   (drew, took, showed)
21. shout, blow, write   (shouted, blew, wrote)
22. get, help, rise   (got, helped, rose)
23. leave, sing, work   (left, sang, worked)
24. ring, like, see   (rang, liked, saw)
25. plant, run, give   (planted, ran, gave)
26. throw, twist, eat   (threw, twisted, ate)
27. know, sit, roar   (knew, sat, roared)
28. stay, grow, give   (stayed, grew, gave)
29. write, reach, begin   (wrote, reached, began)
30. take, come, ask   (took, came, asked)
31. do, need, ride   (did, needed, rode)
32. wait, give, fall   (waited, gave, fell)
33. tear, swim, teach   (tore, swam, taught)
34. wear, sit, jump   (wore, sat, jumped)
35. speak, hope, leave   (spoke, hoped, left)
36. honk, freeze, bring   (honked, froze, brought)
37. choose, scare, fly   (chose, scared, flew)
38. steal, blow, pull   (stole, blew, pulled)
39. break, feel, draw   (broke, felt, drew)
40. pick, drive, leave   (picked, drove, left)
41. hide, lift, raise   (hid, lifted, raised)
42. write, get, trace   (wrote, got, traced)
43. say, yell, take   (said, yelled, took)
44. move, swim, drink   (moved, swam, drank)
45. draw, lie, melt   (drew, lay, melted)

116 PAST TENSE—"HELPING" VERBS

Materials needed
none

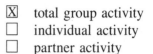

☒ total group activity
☐ individual activity
☐ partner activity

Total Group Activity

Most students need added practice in forming irregular past tenses because they are frequently misused in everyday spoken language. Forming the perfect tense, which requires using "helping" verbs, is even more of a problem because students seldom speak or write these words. Explain that the word *have* is the helping verb that also means *to own or possess* when used by itself.

First have the students practice forming irregular past tenses by reading one of the words from the following list and calling on a student to use the word in a sentence in past tense form. For example:

TAKE—I *took* my book home last night.

When all of the words have been practiced in this form, read the list again, asking students to use the specified word in the perfect tense, that is, with a "helping" verb, for example:

TAKE—I *have taken* the garbage out.

The words in the list are written in the present tense. First the past tense and then the perfect tense follow them in boldface print.

Variation: Read one of the listed words, then specify "past tense" or "helping" verb. Call on a student to use the word in a sentence in the form you requested. For example:

BREAK, helping verb—
I *have broken* all of my crayons.

RUN, past tense—
I *ran* as fast as I could

Form the Past Tense or Use a "Helping" Verb

1. break **(broke, have broken)**
2. come **(came, have come)**
3. grow **(grew, have grown)**
4. catch **(caught, have caught)**
5. give **(gave, have given)**
6. do **(did, have done)**
7. think **(thought, have thought)**
8. take **(took, have taken)**
9. buy **(bought, have bought)**
10. do **(did, have done)**
11. read **(read, have read)**
12. sleep **(slept, have slept)**
13. see **(saw, have seen)**
14. throw **(threw, have thrown)**
15. bring **(brought, have brought)**
16. go **(went, have gone)**
17. run **(ran, have run)**
18. eat **(ate, have eaten)**
19. raise **(raised, have raised)**
20. draw **(drew, have drawn)**
21. steal **(stole, have stolen)**
22. drink **(drank, have drunk)**
23. blow **(blew, have blown)**
24. teach **(taught, have taught)**
25. get **(got, have gotten)**
26. write **(wrote, have written)**
27. choose **(chose, have chosen)**
28. hide **(hid, have hidden)**
29. leave **(left, have left)**
30. freeze **(frozen, have frozen)**
31. tear **(tore, have torn)**
32. fly **(flew, have flown)**
33. wear **(wore, have worn)**
34. begin **(began, have begun)**
35. feel **(felt, have felt)**
36. know **(knew, have known)**
37. rise **(rose, have risen)**
38. drive **(drove, have driven)**
39. swing **(swung, have swung)**
40. fall **(fell, have fallen)**
41. ride **(rode, have ridden)**
42. speak **(spoke, have spoken)**
43. sing **(sang, have sung)**
44. ring **(rang, have rung)**
45. lie **(lay, have lain)**
46. lay **(laid, have laid)**
47. sit **(sat, have sat)**
48. set **(set, have set)**

117   ALPHABETICAL PARTS OF SPEECH

Materials needed

Total Group Activity

Designate a part of speech (noun, verb, adjective, or adverb) and pick a letter of the alphabet (for example: noun—S). Call on a student. By the count of ten, ask for the answer. Raise your fingers one at a time to indicate the count.

If a correct answer is given, the student then names a part of speech and a new letter of the alphabet, and calls on a classmate to respond. If an incorrect answer is given or there is no response by the count of ten, the player continues to be the leader.

However, the student called on may say, "I challenge." In this case, the leader must be able to give a correct answer by the count of ten or the challenger becomes the leader. Students should be encouraged to call on classmates who have not yet had a turn.

118   I'LL SAY THE ADJECTIVE, YOU SAY THE NOUN

Materials needed
dictionary
paper
pencil

☒ total group activity
☐ individual activity
☐ partner activity

Total Group Activity

Read an adjective from the list below and ask the students to name a noun that goes with the adjective. For instance, if you said *vivid*, they might say *dream*. If they are uncertain about the meaning of a word, give a brief definition and then continue with the activity. (Use only the first twenty-five words on the list with younger students.)

Although there are many nouns that could accompany each adjective, ask for one answer only, and specify that nouns cannot be repeated. You or a student should make a list of the words used so that repetitions can be spotted easily. As more and more nouns are eliminated, the level of difficulty increases, which results in a thought-provoking challenge for students.

Give a Noun to Go with—

1. gentle	14. magnificent	27. sympathetic	39. shimmering
2. soiled	15. powerful	28. immense	40. enraged
3. ridiculous	16. spotless	29. fearless	41. despised
4. sparkling	17. ferocious	30. dreadful	42. quivering
5. timid	18. overflowing	31. smudged	43. sweltering
6. cheerful	19. towering	32. dainty	44. exasperated
7. peaceful	20. rapid	33. drenched	45. trivial
8. trembling	21. humorous	34. forlorn	46. parched
9. clever	22. ill-tempered	35. boisterous	47. faint-hearted
10. naughty	23. delicate	36. bleak	48. jubilant
11. reckless	24. dim	37. affectionate	49. rigid
12. spooky	25. flimsy	38. courageous	50. ravenous
13. shrill	26. demolished		

119   VERB PAIRS

Materials needed
none

☒ total group activity
☐ individual activity
☐ partner activity

Total Group Activity

Review verbs with students, making certain they understand that verbs generally denote an action or "doing something."

Read the following pairs of words twice, pausing between readings to give students time to think. They should respond on the signal "Now" by holding up the first two fingers of one hand in a *V* if both are verbs or crossing their arms on their chests if one word is a noun (mismatch). If the words are mismatched, the word that is *not* a verb is given in the answer key.

Variation

Materials needed
lined paper for each student
pencil for each student

Have the students number their papers from one to fifteen. Read each pair of words and have the students write *V* if both words are verbs or *X* if they are a mismatch.

Is It a Verb Pair or a Mismatch?

1. unfasten, straighten	**(match)**	14. dollar, bury	**(mismatch—dollar)**
2. desk, enter	**(mismatch—desk)**	15. introduce, magnet	**(mismatch—magnet)**
3. earn, complain	**(match)**	16. breathe, choose	**(match)**
4. eat, palace	**(mismatch—palace)**	17. fireplace, enjoy	**(mismatch—fireplace)**
5. ask, sit	**(match)**	18. knit, misplace	**(match)**
6. newspaper, save	**(mismatch—newspaper)**	19. join, iceberg	**(mismatch—iceberg)**
7. rob, applaud	**(match)**	20. rub, juggle	**(match)**
8. sing, bake	**(match)**	21. interrupt, thumbtack	**(mismatch—thumbtack)**
9. carpenter, carve	**(mismatch—carpenter)**	22. magazine, crumple	**(mismatch—magazine)**
10. speak, erase	**(match)**	23. appear, celebrate	**(match)**
11. argue, stumble	**(match)**	24. cram, hear	**(match)**
12. obey, tarantula	**(mismatch—tarantula)**	25. bathe, instrument	**(mismatch—instrument)**
13. amuse, breathe	**(match)**		

120   ADJECTIVE OR ADVERB?

Materials needed
chalkboard
chalk
eraser
Optional: clock *or* timer

☒ total group activity
☐ individual activity
☐ partner activity

Total Group Activity

Review adjectives and adverbs with the students. Adjectives tell *what kind, whose, which,* or *how many*. Adverbs tell *how, when,* or *where*.

Divide the class into two teams and number the players. Alternate giving items from the following list to the teams, keeping score on the chalkboard.

Read a pair of words, one of which will be either an adjective or an adverb and the other the word modified. The player identifies the word as an adjective or adverb and explains how it modifies the other word (for example, tells how many, what kind, where, and so on). The word underscored on the list is the adjective or adverb.

Scoring should be handled in the following manner.

1. Team A's answer is correct—Team A earns one point. Play goes to the next player on Team B.

2. Team A's player makes a mistake and the next person on Team B spots the mistake and gives the correct answer—Team B gets the point and continues play.

3. Team A's player makes a mistake and the next player on Team B does not spot the mistake—no points are earned and Team B continues play.

The game ends when all students have had a turn or at the end of a designated time period. The team with the most points wins.

Variation

Materials needed
lined paper for each student
pencil for each student

Have the students number their papers from one to twenty. (Save the other twenty items on the list for another time.) Read each word pair and ask the students to write *adj.* if one of the words is an adjective or *adv.* if one of the words is an adverb.

Is It an Adjective or an Adverb?

1. watched <u>unhappily</u>   **(adverb: how)**
2. <u>affectionate</u> puppy   **(adjective: what kind)**
3. swam <u>yesterday</u>   **(adverb: when)**
4. <u>my</u> umbrella   **(adjective: whose)**
5. stood <u>calmly</u>   **(adverb: how)**
6. folded <u>neatly</u>   **(adverb: how)**
7. <u>angry</u> storekeeper   **(adjective: what kind)**
8. read <u>hurriedly</u>   **(adverb: how)**
9. <u>dismal</u> day   **(adjective: what kind)**
10. <u>several</u> boys   **(adjective: how many)**
11. arrived <u>late</u>   **(adverb: when)**
12. <u>four</u> cousins   **(adjective: how many)**
13. <u>timid</u> mouse   **(adjective: what kind)**
14. arrived <u>unexpectedly</u>   **(adverb: how)**
15. <u>that</u> dog   **(adjective: which)**
16. sat <u>stubbornly</u>   **(adverb: how)**
17. walked <u>downstairs</u>   **(adverb: where)**
18. <u>thirty-three</u> students   **(adjective: how many)**
19. knew <u>instantly</u>   **(adverb: when)**
20. <u>Frank's</u> mother   **(adjective: whose)**
21. <u>freezing</u> weather   **(adjective: what kind)**
22. drove <u>rapidly</u>   **(adverb: how)**
23. <u>these</u> books   **(adjective: which)**
24. sobbed <u>uncontrollably</u>   **(adverb: how)**
25. <u>baseball</u> player   **(adjective: what kind)**
26. <u>many</u> people   **(adjective: how many)**
27. waited <u>anxiously</u>   **(adverb: how)**
28. <u>seldom</u> came   **(adverb: when)**
29. <u>this</u> road   **(adjective: which)**
30. whispered <u>hoarsely</u>   **(adverb: how)**
31. <u>towering</u> mountain   **(adjective: what kind)**
32. answered <u>pleasantly</u>   **(adverb: how)**
33. <u>some</u> fishermen   **(adjective: how many)**
34. <u>reckless</u> driver   **(adjective: what kind)**
35. came <u>today</u>   **(adverb: when)**
36. <u>Dan's</u> bicycle   **(adjective: whose)**
37. held <u>firmly</u>   **(adverb: how)**
38. slept <u>upstairs</u>   **(adverb: where)**
39. <u>nervous</u> actor   **(adjective: what kind)**
40. walked <u>stiffly</u>   **(adverb: how)**

121   YOU ADD THE ENDING

Materials needed
none

☒ total group activity
☐ individual activity
☐ partner activity

Total Group Activity

Before starting this activity, establish the order in which you will call on students. Read one of the following "story starters." Immediately have the first student add *one sentence* to the plot. The story line progresses from student to student with each contributing a sentence until someone brings it to a logical conclusion. You may also intercede at an appropriate moment to suggest that an effective ending be found. Keep the pace quick and lively for full enjoyment of this activity.

Variation: An alternate method is to have a student continue telling the story while you silently count to thirty (or whatever number you feel is appropriate). At the end of the designated time, say "Pass" and the story progresses to the next student.

A. THE HOMELESS KITTEN (Grades K–2)

Snowball was a fluffy little white kitten who wanted a boy or girl to love him more than anything else in the whole world. At night when he fell asleep he would dream about a home of his very own and about saucers of milk. He'd dream that he was cuddled on a warm lap with a little boy or girl petting him. How happy he was in his dream and, oh, how he wished that dream would come true! Finally, one day he said, "I'm going to find myself a boy or a girl to love me. The first thing I'll do is...

B. THE NEW PUPPY (Grades K–3)

Julie had wanted a puppy for as long as she could remember, but her parents said that she would have to wait until she was old enough to take care of it herself. Each year on her birthday she hoped she would get a puppy, but every year her parents said "No, Julie. We think you need to wait a little longer."

On Monday Julie had another birthday. One of the presents was a small box. When she opened it there was a note inside that said "This Saturday we're going to take a ride. We have a surprise for you. Love, Mom and Dad." Julie wished that the surprise would be a puppy, but she didn't want to get her hopes up too much.

Finally Saturday arrived and everyone piled into the car. They drove and drove and then...

C. FLYING SAUCER ADVENTURE (Grades K–3)

Jake looked out in the back yard and couldn't believe his eyes. He stared, looked away, and then stared again. Yes! There in his very own back yard was a flying saucer! It was silver-colored and looked somewhat like a large, shallow bowl that had been turned upside down. There wasn't any light coming from the inside, but the outside glowed in a strange way. Jake was just about to leave the window and dash to the telephone to call his friend Steve, when to his amazement...

D. RAFT CAPER (Grades 3–6)

Sandy and Annette had been friends for as long as either of them could remember. One hot day the girls decided to go down to the river. While they were playing in the water, Sandy said, "I know what we should do! Let's build a raft with that old lumber Dad gave me."

In no time at all, they were hammering away and the raft was taking shape. Soon it was finished and in the water. They decided to float on it along the edge of the river for just a short distance and then pull the raft out of the water and carry it back to where they started. Everything was fine until...

E. HANG GLIDING (Grades 4–6)

I had always wanted to go hang gliding. I kept thinking about how it would feel to float along on the wind currents and look down on the world.

Finally one day I had my chance. One of my friends, Hank, said I could go along with him and he'd show me what to do. At first he had me jump off some mounds of dirt so I could learn how to land. He kept teaching me tricks and before long I was gliding off a little hill. Sometimes I had trouble, but most of the time everything was fine. Then Hank said, "You seem to be O.K. Why don't you try that hill over there." I looked where he was pointing and thought to myself, "Now, that's a *real* hill!"

When I got to the top I could feel my heart pounding. I stopped for a minute and took a deep breath. Then I decided the time had come. I...

F. A MYSTERIOUS NEW WORLD (Grades 4–6)

I kept telling myself, "This has to be a dream. Things like this don't really happen." Yet I knew it wasn't a dream. I was standing there, wide awake as can be, and right beside me were my parents, looking just as amazed as I was.

It had all started when my family and I were on vacation. We'd gotten lost on a back road, but we really weren't worried because my dad was sure the road he had just turned into would take us to the main highway. The road became narrower and narrower, and finally we drove through an area where the trees touched overhead, forming a long tunnel. I had a strange feeling as we drove through the tunnel. As we came out the other side, I suddenly realized we were in a completely different world. And there in front of me...

122   PICTURE WORDS

Materials needed
paper (6″ x 9″ for class book)
pencil

☐ total group activity
☒ individual activity
☐ partner activity

Individual Activity

This activity provides practice in forming compound words, working with prefixes and suffixes, and thinking creatively.

The student thinks of words whose meanings can be illustrated with pictures. On a sheet of paper two pictures may be drawn next to one another to indicate the word. This works especially well with compound words, as shown here.

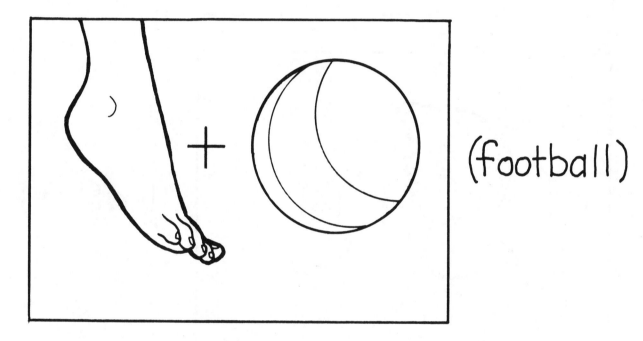

Or a picture may be preceded or followed by a plus sign or minus sign and one or more letters indicating sounds that should be added or deleted, as is seen on p. 174. This works well with prefixes and suffixes.

Answers should be written on the back of the paper. When a sufficient number of "Picture Words" has been collected, assemble them into a booklet to be enjoyed by the class or use them for a bulletin board.

123   CLIMB THE STAIRS

Materials needed
unlined paper
pencil

☐ total group activity
☒ individual activity
☐ partner activity

Individual Activity

This activity builds vocabulary. The student writes words in a "stair" pattern by combining the last letter of a word with the first letter of another word. Initially place no restrictions on the words used. But as the student's skill increases, limit the words to those within a designated category from the list below.

```
room
   o
   t
   h
   e
   rabbit
        e
        l
        e
        p
        h
        o
        n
   elephant
            i
            g
            e
        river
             o
             u
             t
        eraser
```

Word Categories:

animals	nouns
fruits/vegetables	verbs
girls' names	adjectives
boys' names	adverbs
things that make sounds	cities
colors	states
things you can see in the classroom	countries
items found in a house	musical instruments
items found in a kitchen	rivers
ways to get from one place to another	mountains
types of jobs	

124   ALONE WE STAND

Materials needed
lined paper
pencil

☐ total group activity
☒ individual activity
☒ partner activity

Individual Activity

This activity builds vocabulary.

Designate words of a certain length and challenge the student to write as many words as possible in which no letters are repeated. Have a younger student start with four-letter or five-letter words. An upper-grade student can start with six-letter or seven-letter words.

5-letter words
sixth
lemon
black
house

7-letter words
talking
reading
skating
jumping

Variation: Challenge the student to write all of the five-letter or longer words with double consonants that he or she can think of. The doubled letter may be at the beginning, middle, or end of the word. For example: llama, giraffe, recess.

Partner Adaptation

Materials needed
lined paper
pencils
dictionary
clock *or* timer

The students decide on the length of the words they will write and the amount of time they will work on their lists. Each then writes as many words as possible in which no letter is repeated. A dictionary is used to check spelling. The student who writes the most correctly spelled words within the time limit wins.

125   LITTLE WORDS FROM BIG WORDS

Materials needed
lined paper
pencil

☐ total group activity
☒ individual activity
☒ partner activity

Individual Activity

This activity builds vocabulary and gives practice in creative thinking.

On the chalkboard write one of the words from the following list. The student forms as many words as possible using only the letters in the designated word. Proper names, foreign words, and plural forms of the same word are not allowed.

Specify that a letter from the designated word may not be used twice in the same new word. For instance, if the stem word were *beautiful*, the *l* could not be repeated to form the word *fill*.

beautiful
tea
bite
fit
bit
life

Partner Adaptation

Materials needed
lined paper
pencils
dictionary
clock *or* timer

Partners write the same word at the top of their papers. They each write as many words as they can that are composed of letters from the chosen word. At the end of an agreed upon time, a dictionary is used to check spelling. The player with the most correctly spelled words wins.

Form as Many Words as You Can from This Word—

1. basketball
2. gingerbread
3. somersault
4. doughnut
5. hippopotamus
6. television
7. snowmobile
8. helicopter
9. constellation
10. grandmother
11. chalkboard
12. handwriting
13. scarecrow
14. caterpillar
15. photograph
16. supermarket
17. instrument
18. lemonade
19. temperature
20. experiment

126   HIDDEN WORD PUZZLE

Materials needed
graph paper
pencil

☐ total group activity
☒ individual activity
☒ partner activity

Individual Activity

This activity builds vocabulary and gives practice in creative thinking.

The student writes words from a selected category in a crossword puzzle format on a piece of graph paper, placing one letter within each square. The same words are listed on the back of the paper to serve as an answer key. When no more words from the category will fit, miscellaneous letters of the alphabet are written in the remaining empty squares.

Designate a place for students to put their completed papers so they can be used as challenges for classmates. When students work on the puzzles, have them write their answers on a separate piece of paper so that the puzzles can be reused.

e								
l	e	o	p	a	r	d		
e								
p					a	d		
h	a	n	t	e	l	o	p	e
a		i	a	i		e	e	
n		g	g	o			r	
t		e	l	n				
		r	e					

answers:
elephant
leopard
antelope
tiger
eagle
lion
ape
deer

Partner Adaptation

Materials needed
graph paper
pencils
clock *or* timer

Each partner secretly writes words from a selected category in a crossword puzzle format on graph paper, placing one letter in each square. When no more words will fit, any letter of the alphabet is written in each of the remaining squares. The answers are written on a separate piece of paper.

Partners exchange papers and circle as many of the hidden words as possible within an agreed-upon time limit. The student who designed the puzzle receives one point for each word his or her opponent does *not* locate. The player with the most points wins.

127 VOWEL DETECTIVE

Materials needed
lined paper
pencils

☐ total group activity
☐ individual activity
☒ partner activity

Partner Activity

This activity provides practice in phonics and spelling.

The partners decide how many words they will write in a puzzle sentence. Suggest that they start with five-word sentences and increase the length as their skill increases.

Each student secretly writes a sentence of the designated length. This serves as an answer sheet. The students recopy their sentences but replace each vowel with a dash. For example:

Is your homework finished?
__s y__ __r h__m__w__rk f__n__sh__d?

fold

This is my new record.
Th__s __s m__ n__w r__c__rd.

Students fold the answer section under and exchange papers. The first student to decode the partner's sentence receives one point. New sentences are written and the process is repeated until one of the students has accumulated five points.

Variation: Students may elect to remove all vowels and dashes to make the decoding task more difficult.

128   CATEGORY PLOT

Materials needed
lined paper
pencil
Optional: ruler

☐ total group activity
☒ individual activity
☒ partner activity

Individual activity

This activity provides practice in spelling and creative thinking.

The student writes a word vertically down the left-hand margin of paper, one letter per line. For example, the word *family* is shown on the left. The rest of the paper is divided into four columns with a category written at the top of each. A list of possible categories is provided below. The student thinks of a word for each category that begins with the letter in the left-hand margin.

	animals	colors	adjectives	adverbs
f	fox		favorite	
a	ant		aching	
m	monkey	mauve		mildly
i	ibex	ivory		
l	lion	lilac	little	loudly
y	yak	yellow		

Partner Adaptation

Materials needed
lined paper
pencils
dictionary
clock *or* timer

Partners agree on a time limit. They then decide on a word, which is written by both students vertically down the left-hand margin of a piece of paper. The rest of their papers are divided into four columns. Partners alternate naming categories and both write these at the column tops on their papers. Working independently, the students think of a word for every category that begins with the letter in the left-hand margin. At the end of the allotted time, a dictionary is used to check spelling. One point is awarded for each *letter* in correctly spelled words. The student with the most points wins.

Word Categories

animals	items in a house	cities
fruits/vegetables	types of jobs	states
girls' names	nouns	countries
boys' names	verbs	musical instruments
things that make sounds	adjectives	rivers
colors	adverbs	mountains

129   WANDERING WORDS

Materials needed
unlined paper *or* graph paper
pencil
Optional: ruler

☐ total group activity
☒ individual activity
☒ partner activity

Individual Activity

This activity provides spelling practice and builds vocabulary.

The student draws a grid with twenty-five squares. One letter of the alphabet is randomly written in each square. An extra *e* and another letter of the student's choice should be substituted for the letter *q* and *z*.

The student tries to find and write as many words as possible with three letters or more, starting with any letter on the grid and moving from square to square, horizontally, vertically, or diagonally. Only letters that touch each other in order may be used, and letters may be used only once in a word. Proper names may not be used and plurals do not count as extra words. An example is shown here.

e	c	e	i	j
k	a	l	g	f
t	u	b	s	y
d	m	g	e	r
w	o	n	m	h

table
take
hem
gone
won
done
money

Partner Adaptation

Materials needed
paper *or* graph paper
pencils
dictionary
Optional: ruler
clock *or* timer

Each partner draws a twenty-five-square grid and writes a letter of the alphabet in each square. One extra *e* plus one extra letter of each student's choice is substituted for *q* and *z*.

Within an agreed-upon time limit, students work independently, writing as many three-letter or longer words as they can find by starting at any square and moving from square to square, horizontally, vertically, or diagonally. Only letters that touch each other in order may be used, and letters may be used only once in a word. Proper names may not be used and plurals do not count as extra words. At the end of the allotted time a dictionary is used to check spellings. One point is scored for each correctly spelled word. The student with the most points wins.

130   GHOST

Materials needed
paper
pencils
dictionary

☐ total group activity
☐ individual activity
☒ partner activity

Partner Activity

This activity provides spelling practice, builds vocabulary, and helps develop strategy.

The first player writes a letter. The other student thinks of a word that begins with the designated letter and writes the second letter of the word. Players continue to alternate writing letters, trying *not* to be the person who completes a word that is four or more letters in length. Proper names, foreign words, and abbreviations may not be used.

Words of one, two, or three letters do not count against a player. However, the first time a student writes a letter that completes a word of four or more letters, he or she receives a *G*, the next time an *H*, and so on, until the word *GHOST* is spelled. The first player with *GHOST* loses the game.

If a player thinks the opponent wrote a letter that is not part of a real word, the player says, "I challenge." If the other student cannot give a real word or misspells the intended word, he or she loses that round and receives the next letter in *GHOST*. However, if the player *can* give an appropriate word, the challenger loses the round and is "awarded" the next letter. A dictionary is used when the spelling of a word is questioned.

131   HANGMAN

Materials needed
paper
pencils

☐ total group activity
☐ individual activity
☒ partner activity

Partner Activity

This activity gives spelling practice, builds vocabulary, and helps to develop strategy.

Player 1 draws a picture of gallows, writes the letters of the alphabet across the top of the paper, then thinks of a word and writes a dash for each letter in that word. You may want to stipulate that the chosen word be from a current unit of study or from a particular subject (science, history, and so on), or is a specific part of speech (verb, noun, and so on).

Player 2 guesses a letter of the alphabet and crosses it off. If it is one of the letters in the chosen word, Player 1 writes it on the correct dash. If the letter appears more than once, it is written in all places.

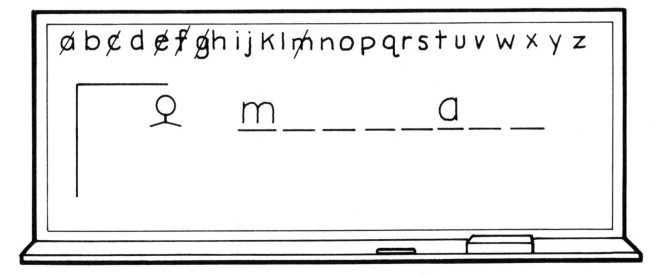

If the player guesses a letter that is not in the word, the head of a stick figure is drawn, just below the gallows. With each wrong guess, another part of the stick figure is added as follows:

1. head
2. neck
3. arms (one at a time)
4. hands (one at a time)
5. body
6. legs (one at a time)
7. feet (one at a time)

With the final incorrect guess, the connecting link between the gallows and the stick figure is drawn. The object of the game is for Player 2 to guess the word before this happens. If the student succeeds, he or she wins the game and chooses the word for the next round. Otherwise, Player 1 continues.

132   SIMPLIFIED CROSSWORD PUZZLE

Materials needed:
lined paper
pencil

☐ total group activity
☒ individual activity
☐ partner activity

Individual Activity

This activity provides spelling practice, builds vocabulary, and gives writing practice.

A word of six letters or more is written with one letter beneath the other, and each is numbered as shown here. A box is then drawn around the word. The student writes a five-letter or longer word that begins with each of the letters in the original word. This becomes the answer sheet.

```
1. |F| E N C E
2. |O| R A N G E
3. |R| A Z O R
4. |G| A R A G E
5. |E| L E P H A N T
6. |T| E L E P H O N E
```

On the reverse side of the paper the numbers are copied and dashes written in place of the letters. A box is drawn around the first dash in all of the words. A crossword puzzle-type clue is then written for each word.

1. |‾| _ _ _ _
2. |‾| _ _ _ _ _
3. |‾| _ _ _ _
4. |‾| _ _ _ _ _
5. |‾| _ _ _ _ _ _ _
6. |‾| _ _ _ _ _ _ _

1. This helps to keep animals in their own yard.
2. The color of carrots.

Designate a place for students to put completed papers so they can be used as challenges for their classmates. When a student works a puzzle, his or her answers should be written on a separate piece of paper so the original puzzle can be reused.

133   ALLITERATION DAZE

Materials needed
lined paper
pencil

☐ total group activity
☒ individual activity
☐ partner activity

Individual Activity

This activity provides spelling and writing practice, and builds vocabulary.

The student writes the letters of the alphabet vertically in the left-hand margin of a piece of paper, skipping two lines between each. He or she chooses a topic such as, "I have...." For every letter of the alphabet, the student tries to think of a sentence in which almost all of the words begin with the designated letter. For example:

a	I have an active anteater who eats aggravated ants.
b	I have a big bright bee who buzzes busily beneath berry bushes.
c	....

Variation: The student uses the topic "I went to _____(the name of a place)." For example:

I went to California to catch a camel
carrying a cargo of carrots.

134   FLIP-FLOP WORDS

Materials needed
lined paper
pencils
dictionary
clock *or* timer

☐ total group activity
☒ individual activity
☒ partner activity

Partner Activity

This activity provides spelling practice, builds vocabulary, and develops creative thinking.

Partners select a word of four letters or more, depending on the age and ability level of the students. Each student writes the word vertically on the left-hand side of the paper and vertically *in reverse order* on the right-hand side of the paper as shown here.

Students then try to fill in words on each line that begin with the letter on the left and end with the letter on the right.

f	finds	s
l	later	r
o	owe	e
w	wow	w
e	ego	o
r	real	l
s	self	f

Before filling in the words, the partners set a time limit. At the end of the designated time the papers are exchanged. A dictionary is used to check spelling. For each word spelled correctly, the student receives one point. The student with the most points wins.

Adaptation for an Individual Student

Materials needed
lined paper
pencil
dictionary
clock *or* timer

Follow the above directions and have the individual student try to fill in as many words as possible within a given time limit.

135   FILL IN THE BLANK

Materials needed
chalkboard
chalk
lined paper
pencil

Individual Activity

This activity provides spelling practice, builds vocabulary, and develops creative thinking.

Write several beginning/ending letter combinations on the chalkboard using the list below. Explain that two or more common four-letter words can be made from each combination and that ten or more can be made from some of the letter combinations. For example:

> p–l: pull
>
> peel
>
> peal
>
> pill
>
> pool
>
> pail

Challenge each student to write as many words as he or she can for each of the letter combinations.

Letter Combinations

h–e	b–d	p–l
m–e	w–t	t–l
r–e	m–t	s–e
l–e	c–t	r–t

136   WORD TO WORD TO WORD

Materials needed
paper (6″ x 9″ for class book)
pencil

☐   total group activity
☒   individual activity
☐   partner activity

Individual Activity

This activity provides spelling practice, builds vocabulary, and develops creative thinking.

The student writes a three- or four-letter word and then changes one letter to form a new word. The new word is written beneath the first one and then another letter in a *different position* is changed. This continues until the original word has been changed three times for a three-letter word or four times for a four-letter word.

The paper is turned over and a brief riddle is written on the other side telling the original word, the number of changes, and the final word. For example:

Start with <u>rode</u>. Make 4 changes and you'll have <u>wish</u>	rode rose rise wise wish

Designate a place for students to put completed papers so that they can be used as challenges for others. Or assemble the papers into a "Word to Word to Word" class puzzle book.

137   BUILD A PYRAMID

Materials needed
paper (6″ x 9″ for class book)
pencil
Optional: ruler

☐   total group activity
☒   individual activity
☐   partner activity

Individual Activity

This activity provides spelling practice, builds vocabulary, and develops creative thinking.

The student draws the pyramid shown below. At the top he or she writes a single letter. In the space below, the letter is repeated and a new letter is added to form a two-letter word. A new letter is added in this way on each level of the pyramid. The sequence of the previous letters may be shifted or may remain the same. This process continues until the final five-letter word is written.

You can assemble the papers into a "Build a Pyramid" class puzzle book if you wish.

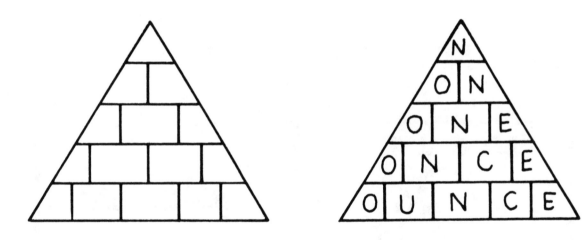

138   I C U!

Materials needed
paper (6″ x 9″ for class book)
pencil (pen for class book)

☐ total group activity
☒ individual activity
☐ partner activity

Individual Activity

This activity provides writing practice and develops creative thinking.

Many numerals and letters of the alphabet, either alone or combined, sound like words in the English language. For example:

C (see or sea)
4 (for)
L N (Ellen)
I (eye)
C T (city)

In this activity the student thinks of a statement that may be expressed using letters and/or numbers and writes it on a piece of paper. The saying should also be illustrated to help convey the meaning. The actual sentence is then written on the reverse side as an answer key.

When you have collected a sufficient number of papers, assemble them into a class puzzle book to be enjoyed by all.

The book *C D B!*, by William Stein (New York: Simon & Schuster, 1968), is a delightful complement to the above activity.

139   LETTER SWAP

Materials needed
paper (6″ x 9″ for class book)
pencil

☐   total group activity
☒   individual activity
☐   partner activity

Individual Activity

This activity provides spelling practice, builds vocabulary, and develops creative thinking.

Challenge the student to find a word that becomes a new word when one letter is changed. The sequence of the other letters may be shifted or may remain the same. For example:

maple—Change one letter and it becomes *apple*.
read—Change one letter and it becomes *pear*.

The student writes the initial word on one side of a piece of paper and a clue indicating the category in which the word will belong when one letter is changed. The answer is then written on the reverse side. As many of these "Letter Swap" puzzles as desired may be made. Several may be assembled into a challenging class puzzle book for individual or whole-class use.

Change one letter in the word *bread* and you'll have a zoo animal.

ANSWER: Zebra

140   HINK PINK

Materials needed
paper (6″ x 9″ for class book)
pencil

☐   total group activity
☒   individual activity
☐   partner activity

Individual Activity

This activity builds vocabulary because students must search for words that offer precise definitions. A Hink Pink is composed of two one-syllable rhyming words that make sense together. For example:

no dough

The clue for the Hink Pink can be written as a synonym or as a statement. For example:

no dough:

zero money

What you'll have if you spend all your money.

If the rhyming answer consists of two two-syllable words, it is called a Hinky Pinky. Two three-syllable words make a Hinkety Pinkety.

The student writes a clue on one side of a piece of paper and the answer on the reverse side. When a sufficient number of these have been collected, assemble them into a book to be used as a challenge for individuals or the whole class.

141   SCRAMBLED ORAL SENTENCES

Materials needed
none

☒ total group activity
☐ individual activity
☐ partner activity

Total Group Activity

Read a sentence from the following list in which one word is in the wrong place. Have students raise their hands when they decide how the sentence should have been worded. Then call on a volunteer to repeat it correctly. The misplaced word appears in boldface type in the following sentences and its correct placement is shown within parentheses.

Unscramble This

1. The boys **across** raced (across) the field.
2. My friend and I played baseball **school** after (school) yesterday.
3. On our vacation **summer** last (summer), my family went on a long hike.
4. Did your football (team) win its game **team** last night?
5. My **thing** puppy is the cutest (thing) you ever saw.
6. What is the **interesting** most (interesting) book you ever read?
7. I'm going to play soccer (after) school this afternoon **after**.
8. Frank got a new ten **bike** speed (bike) for his birthday.
9. I love **fire** to sit in front of a (fire) on a cold winter day.
10. What is **favorite** your (favorite) thing to do during the summer?
11. Does your sister (go) to the junior high school **go**?
12. It's **made** hard to believe that paper is (made) from wood.
13. Do **remember** you (remember) when you learned to tell time?
14. I hope my (family) gets to go skiing this **family** winter.
15. Can you come over **my** to (my) house after school today?
16. **Interesting** there are many (interesting) things to do with a computer.
17. I **this** overslept (this) morning and was almost late for school.
18. Tom wanted to know **many** how (many) children there were in our family.
19. A bear walked (right) by our tent while we were **right** camping.
20. What are **going** you (going) to be for Halloween this year?
21. Did you see that great movie (on) TV last **on** night?
22. Do you like to hold **breath** your (breath) when you go through a tunnel?
23. How **house** many people were at your (house) for Thanksgiving dinner?
24. I **believe** couldn't (believe) it was time for school to start again!
25. Dad said we have a **somewhere** mouse (somewhere) in the kitchen.
26. I saw the funniest (car) on the way to school this **car** morning.
27. It's fun to watch the shape of clouds and see if **look** they (look) like an animal or a person.
28. I have a **school** lot of homework to do after (school) today.
29. Which **worse** is (worse), very hot weather or very cold weather?
30. When the firecrackers exploded my dog (ran) and sat right **ran** by me.

142   SPOT THE MISTAKE

Materials needed
none

[X]   total group activity
[ ]   individual activity
[ ]   partner activity

Total Group Activity

Explain that each of the sentences you are going to read from the following list has a mistake in it. The students are to listen for the mistake and decide how to correct it. A student will then be called on to say the entire sentence correctly.

If students have difficulty repeating the entire sentence, begin the activity by having them mentally identify the incorrect word. When called upon, they need only say the word that should have been used in the sentence. Then progress to having students say the entire sentence correctly.

For each sentence the incorrect word is printed in boldface type and the correct word follows it in parentheses. While these answers are the likely ones, accept differing answers if the students can back them with good reasoning.

Variation: This activity can be used to increase student vocabulary by occasionally stopping after a sentence and discussing the meaning of the correct word.

Spot the Mistake

1. During the summer we checked the **barometer (thermometer)** every day to see how hot it was.
2. The squirrel **flurried (scurried)** up the tree.
3. They spent a **peasant (pleasant)** day at the beach.
4. During the storm there were brilliant flashes in the sky and we heard the **lightning (thunder)**.
5. The park bench had a **signal (sign)** on it that said "Wet Paint."
6. At the county fair I always try to **perch (pitch)** coins into the glass cups and saucers.
7. The bowl didn't break when I dropped it, because it was **elastic (plastic)**.
8. When it gets very cold, water starts to **melt (freeze)**.
9. She began to **seep (weep)** when she heard the bad news.
10. By reading the information in the **newscaster (newspaper)**, I found the answer.
11. The turkey was **stuttered (stuffed)** with dressing.
12. While Tom was making a cake, he upset the bowl and spilled the **lather (batter)**.
13. Father said, "We can't wait all day, so you'll have to make an **incision (decision)** about where you want to go."
14. When you rub your hands together very fast, they get warm because of the **fraction (friction)**.
15. When the deer looked into the water, he saw his **inflection (reflection)**.
16. If you let water stay in an open dish, after awhile it will all **elongate (evaporate)**.
17. If you want to have good friends, be certain to **exclude (include)** them whenever you're doing something interesting.
18. Bees are **distracted (attracted)** to flowers.
19. They went on a long **jury (journey)** from their home.

20. He was a very good **author (artist)** who had painted many pictures.

21. When John heard about the collection for the poor people, he wanted to make a **constitution (contribution)**.

22. Winter was on the way, so it was time for the birds to start **hibernating (migrating)**.

23. It takes many weeks of **dispersal (rehearsal)** to put on a play.

24. When passengers get off a plane, you can meet them at the **departure (arrival)** gate.

25. It is important to have good manners and to **inspect (respect)** people who are older than you.

26. If you concentrate on what you are doing, you will **enumerate (eliminate)** many mistakes.

27. It was so cold he began to **shrink (shiver)**.

28. After the ball hit Jake in the stomach, he **stammered (staggered)** across the field.

29. It is important to **detract (subtract)** carefully when you take one number away from another.

30. This year there was a bumper crop of apples from that **orchid (orchard)**.

31. We cooked the steaks in the **boiler (broiler)**.

32. The quality of her work is so good that she always gets an **inferior (superior)** rating.

33. Bill had good manners, so he always made a good **depression (impression)** on everyone he met.

34. Our seasons are caused by the earth's **agitation (rotation)** around the sun.

35. The date on his driver's license had **retired (expired)**, so he needed to get a new license.

36. The fish is caught once the hook is **settled (set)**.

37. The television **commander (commentator)** made an interesting comment after the President's speech.

38. When there is a drought, everyone must **reverse (conserve)** water.

39. It was hard to **congeal (conceal)** the large weapon.

40. Put the chairs back in the proper **rotation (location)**.

41. He tried to **refuse (rescue)** the person from drowning.

42. All the animals were **disclosed (enclosed)** in a huge pen.

43. We should all **reside (abide)** by the rules of our school.

44. What **rejection (objection)** could anyone have to people having a good time?

45. Please climb up the ladder and come **overboard (aboard)** the ship.

143   LOOK AT ME!

Materials needed
none

[X] total group activity
[ ] individual activity
[ ] partner activity

Total Group Activity

Students sit on their chairs, which have been moved about an arm's length in back of their desks. Remaining seated with eyes closed, they follow the series of directions below (for example: "cross arms, wiggle nose, put hands on hips"). The final instruction is "Freeze. You should be in this position." Slowly read the position to the children and have them check to see if they are in the position you describe.

Variation: Rather than using the entire series of directions with younger students, you may want to stop partway through. For this reason, a description of the students' position is given after the tenth instruction. (If your students enjoyed this activity, "Rest Your Chin on Your Chest," (p. 198) is a similar exercise in following a series of directions.)

Oral Directions

1. Look at me and remain seated.
2. Close your eyes.
3. Cross your ankles.
4. Put your hands over your eyes.
5. Wiggle your nose.
6. Put your hands on your hips.
7. Rest your chin on your chest.
8. Stretch your hands out in front of you.
9. Wiggle your fingers.
10. Keeping your hands stretched out in front of you, point your fingers to the floor.
    (If you stop at this point, say "Freeze. You should be in this position.")
    (POSITION: Sitting, eyes closed, ankles crossed, chin on chest, hands extended forward with fingers pointed toward floor.)
11. Put your right hand on your left knee.
12. Put your left hand on your right shoulder.
13. Put your chin on your right shoulder.
14. Bend forward.
15. Put your chin on your left shoulder.
16. Freeze. You should be in this position.
    (POSITION: Sitting, eyes closed, ankles crossed, chin on left shoulder, right hand on left knee, left hand on right shoulder, and body bent forward.)

144 LISTEN AND DRAW

Materials needed
sheet of unlined paper for each student
pencil for each student

☒ total group activity
☐ individual activity
☐ partner activity

Total Group Activity

Read the following set of directions and have students follow them on a sheet of unlined paper. An answer key is provided below.

Listen and Draw—

1. In the middle of the page draw a triangle.
2. Inside the triangle draw a circle.
3. Inside the circle draw a square.
4. At the top of the paper draw four squares side by side.
5. Draw a circle around the outside of the first square on the left.
6. Put an *X* inside the second square from the left.
7. Draw a triangle inside the third square from the left.
8. Draw a larger square around the fourth square from the left.
9. At the bottom of the page draw a straight line going from left to right.
10. Write your name on the line.
11. Above your name draw a rectangle.
12. Draw a circle just above and touching the rectangle.
13. Divide the circle in half by drawing a line from the top to the bottom.
14. Put dots inside the right-hand side of the circle.
15. Put tiny *X*'s inside the left-hand side of the circle.

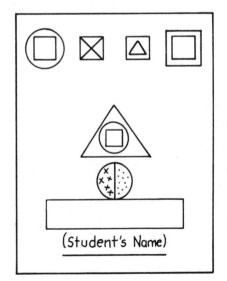

145   REST YOUR CHIN ON YOUR CHEST

Materials needed
none

☒ total group activity
☐ individual activity
☐ partner activity

Total Group Activity

Students sit on their chairs, which have been moved about an arm's length in back of their desks. Remaining seated with eyes closed, they follow the series of directions below (for example: "stand up, twist body to the right, put left hand on right hand"). The final instruction is "Freeze. You should be in this position." Slowly read the position to the children and have them check to see if they are in the position you describe.

Variation: Rather than using the entire series of directions with younger students, you may want to stop halfway through. For this reason, a description of the students' position is given after the tenth instruction.

Oral Directions

1. Rest your chin on your chest and remain seated.
2. Close your eyes.
3. Raise your head and point your face toward me.
4. Put your hands on your waist.
5. Stand up.
6. Twist your body to the right.
7. Put your left hand on your right hand.
8. Twist your body so that it is facing forward again.
9. Nod your head four times.
10. Bend over at the waist.

   (If you stop at this point, say, "Freeze. You should be in this position.")
   (POSITION: Standing, eyes closed, body bent over at waist, right hand on hip, and left hand on top of right hand.)

11. Put your right hand behind your neck.
12. Put your left hand on top of your right hand.
13. Stand up straight.
14. Put your right hand on your left elbow.
15. Put your left hand on your right ear.
16. Freeze. You should be in this position.

   (POSITION: Standing straight, eyes closed, right hand on left elbow, left hand on right ear.)

146   MYSTERY SENTENCE

Materials needed
none

☒ total group activity
☐ individual activity
☐ partner activity

Total Group Activity

For each of the two activities below, have the students write the designated words on their papers. Then ask them to follow the directions you read from the list below. If everything is done correctly, they will have two humorous messages on their papers when they are finished.

Activity 1

BLUBBER BASEMENT BIKES ROOT HIGHLIGHTS!

1. In the first word change *BL* to *R*.
2. Cross out *BASE* and write *CE* at the beginning of the second word.
3. Change *BI* to *MA* in the third word.
4. In the fourth word change *T* to *P*, then rewrite the word in reverse order.
5. Change *LIGHTS* to *WAYS* in the last word.

ANSWER KEY:

R   CE   MA   P   W A Y S
B̷L̷UBBER B̷A̷S̷E̷MENT B̷I̷KES ROOT̷ HIGHL̷I̷G̷H̷T̷S̷!
                                    POOR

(Rubber cement makes poor highways!)

Activity 2

PAY HOG'S BONE KISS HORSE FAN HISTORY BACK!

1. In the first word cross out the first and last letters.
2. In the second word change *H* to *D*.
3. Change *ON* in the third word to *IT*.
4. Cross out the first and last letters in the fourth word. Put a box around the remaining word.
5. In the fifth word change *H* to *W*.
6. Change *F* to *TH* in the sixth word.
7. Cross off the last four letters in the seventh word.
8. Change *C* to *R* in the last word.

ANSWER KEY:

        D   IT   W   TH   R
P̷AY̷ H̷OG'S BO̷N̷E K̷IS̷S̷ H̷ORSE F̷AN HIST̷O̷R̷Y̷ BAC̷K!

(A dog's bite *is* worse than his bark!)

147 GEOMETRIC JUMBLE

Materials needed
sheet of unlined paper for each student
pencil for each student
ruler

☒ total group activity
☐ individual activity
☐ partner activity

Total Group Activity

Before beginning this activity review inches and half inches with the class. Then have the students follow the directions below as you read them. An answer key is provided.

Geometric Jumble Directions

1. In the center of the paper, draw a triangle that is one and a half inches in height.
2. Above the triangle, at the top of the paper, write the letter *A*.
3. One inch below the triangle, going from left to right, draw a zigzag line three inches in length.
4. One-half inch beneath the zigzag line, draw another zigzag line of the same length.
5. Draw a vertical line to connect the beginning points of both zigzag lines.
6. Draw a vertical line to connect the ending points of both zigzag lines.
7. Draw a rectangle around the letter *A*.
8. Color the rectangle.
9. Draw a triangle slightly above and to the left of the first triangle.
10. Draw four small squares between the two zigzag lines, making each square touch the two lines.
11. Color the two triangles.
12. Draw a triangle slightly above and to the right of the first triangle.
13. Color the four small rectangles and the remaining triangle.
14. Starting at the bottom of the rectangle *A*, draw a circle that goes completely around the triangles and zigzag lines.

ANSWER KEY:

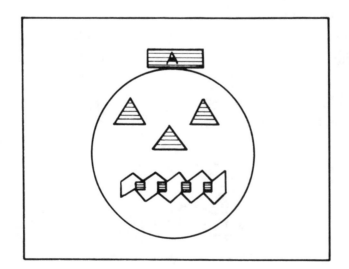

148   I PACKED MY SUITCASE

Materials needed
none

☒ total group activity
☐ individual activity
☐ partner activity

Total Group Activity

The students start with the phrase, "I packed my suitcase and in it I put _____." The first student names one item that might go in a suitcase (for example: "my bathing suit"). The next student repeats the previous statement and adds one more item (for example: "I packed my suitcase and in it I put my bathing suit and shoes.") The turn passes from one student to the nearest student, with each person repeating everything that was said previously and adding one additional item. Challenge the students to see how many items they can name before a mistake is made.

Variation: Students use the phrase, "I'm going to the store to buy _____." Items may be named in random order or you can specify that they must be named in alphabetical order (apples, bananas, carrots, and so on).

149 YOU TELL ME AND I'LL TELL YOU

Materials needed
none

☒ total group activity
☐ individual activity
☐ partner activity

Total Group Activity

Determine the order in which students will take turns. Have them give *one* piece of information about themselves, such as their birthdate (with or without the year of birth), their address, where they were born, and so on. The information is repeated by the next person who then adds his or her own information. Only the previous person's and current person's data is given each time. For example:

Nancy: My birthdate is April 21.

Susan: Nancy's birthdate is April 21.
            My birthdate is October 31.

Jim: Susan's birthdate is October 31.
            My birthdate is February 7.

Students become very involved listening to the information given and determining whether or not it was repeated correctly. Challenge them to try to make the rounds of the entire class without making any mistakes.

150   EXPANDING SENTENCES

Materials needed
none

☒ total group activity
☐ individual activity
☐ partner activity

Total Group Activity

This activity is designed to challenge students' listening abilities.

Read a short sentence from the list below and have a student repeat it. Read the same sentence again, but with an addition to make it longer. Continue to add to the sentence until it has been read and repeated four different times.

You may want to select one student to repeat all of the variations of the same sentence, or you may prefer to rotate the activity among the students. The latter is especially fun if students are seated in rows or in a circle. When someone makes a mistake the same sentence "passes on" to the next person (without being read again) and continues from student to student until someone repeats it correctly. The next expanding sentence is then read and the game continues as above.

When the fourth expansion is said correctly you may want to ask if any other students would like to repeat it. After several repetitions you will find that some of the less secure students begin to volunteer. This results in keeping everyone involved in the activity and promoting a feeling of success for all.

1. We heard a huge lion roar.

   We heard a huge lion roar his loudest roar.

   We heard a huge lion roar his loudest roar at the zoo.

   We heard a huge lion roar his loudest roar at the zoo when the attendant came to feed him.

2. I saw a scrawny cat.

   I saw a scrawny cat lick its paws and clean itself.

   I saw a scrawny cat lick its paws and clean itself while sitting on the fence in my back yard.

   I saw a scrawny cat lick its paws and clean itself while sitting on the fence in my back yard yesterday afternoon.

3. Last night I went to a football game.

   Last night I went to a football game at the high school.

   Last night I went to a football game at the high school and saw my brother's team play.

   Last night I went to a football game at the high school and saw my brother's team play their best game of the season.

4. My baby sister is sleeping in her room.

   My baby sister is sleeping in her room and everything is very quiet.

   My baby sister is sleeping in her room and everything is very quiet, except for the cars driving down the street.

   My baby sister is sleeping in her room and everything is very quiet, except for the cars driving down the street and the fire siren.

5. We have a great soccer team.

   We have a great soccer team that practices after school every day.

   We have a great soccer team that practices after school every day until it is dinner time.

   We have a great soccer team that practices after school every day until it is dinner time and we all have to go home.

6. This morning on my way to school I saw a dog.

   This morning on my way to school I saw a dog chasing a boy.

   This morning on my way to school I saw a dog chasing a boy down the street.

   This morning on my way to school I saw a dog chasing a boy down the street, around a house, and over a fence.

7. We watched a monkey.

   We watched a monkey who was playing hide-and-go-seek with another monkey.

   We watched a monkey who was playing hide-and-go-seek with another monkey yesterday afternoon.

   We watched a monkey who was playing hide-and-go-seek with another monkey yesterday afternoon at the zoo.

8. I like to sail on the lake.

   I like to sail on the lake with several of my friends.

   I like to sail on the lake with several of my friends every Saturday afternoon.

   I like to sail on the lake with several of my friends every Saturday afternoon during the summer.

9. The trees were beautiful.

   The trees were beautiful with red, orange, and golden leaves.

   The trees were beautiful with red, orange, and golden leaves that gently floated to the ground.

   The trees were beautiful with red, orange, and golden leaves that gently floated to the ground whenever the wind blew.

10. I like to swim in a pool.

    I like to swim in a pool with my friends.

    I like to swim in a pool with my friends in my back yard.

    I like to swim in a pool with my friends in my back yard on a hot summer's evening.

151   THE TEACHER'S CAT

Materials needed
none

☒ total group activity
☐ individual activity
☐ partner activity

Total Group Activity

Decide on the order in which students will take turns. A student starts this activity by rhythmically saying, "The teacher's cat is an ———— cat" using an adjective beginning with the letter *a* to describe the cat. The next person repeats the sentence using an adjective that begins with *b*, and so on through the alphabet. Challenge the students to see how far they can go before breaking the rhythm or making a mistake. For example:

The teacher's cat is an active cat.

The teacher's cat is a beautiful cat.

The teacher's cat is a curious cat.

The teacher's cat is a delicate cat.

I'M QUITE A CAT!

152   CAN YOU DRAW MY DESIGN?

Materials needed
unlined paper
pencils

☐   total group activity
☐   individual activity
☒   partner activity

Partner Activity

This activity develops listening skills.

Each partner secretly draws a simple geometric design. You may want to specify the number of shapes that can be used. One of the students then describes his or her design without pointing or using hand motions. Students should decide whether the "direction giver" may watch the partner reproduce the drawing, or whether it should be drawn in secret. Secrecy can be easily accomplished by standing a couple of open books in front of the paper.

Students reverse roles when the drawing has been guessed.

153   BURIED TREASURE

Materials needed
unlined paper
pencils

☐ total group activity
☐ individual activity
☒ partner activity

Partner Activity

This activity develops listening skills.

Each partner draws a buried treasure map, but does *not* indicate on the map where the treasure is buried. The location is secretly written on a separate piece of paper or on the back of the map. (For example: The treasure is located just to the right of the large tree.)

As both students look at one map, the "map drawer" describes how to get to the buried treasure. The "treasure seeker" mentally follows the directions. When all of the directions have been given, the "map drawer" announces, "You should now be at the treasure." The "treasure seeker" indicates where he or she will begin digging, and the "map drawer" tells whether or not the "treasure seeker" will be successful.

Students then reverse roles.